More Secrets of
Happy Children

More Secrets of Happy Children

Steve Biddulph

with Shaaron Biddulph

HARPER
thorsons

This edition produced for The Book People Ltd,
Hall Wood Avenue, Haydock, St Helens WA11 9UL

Thorsons
An Imprint of HarperCollins*Publishers*
77–85 Fulham Palace Road,
Hammersmith, London W6 8JB

The website address is:
www.thorsonselement.com

First published in Australia as a BayBooks Publication in 1994
This edition published by Thorsons 1999
This printing 2007

© Steve and Shaaron Biddulph 1994, 1998

Steve and Shaaron Biddulph assert their moral right to
be identified as the authors of this work.

Cover design: Miller Hare
Illustrations by Paul Stanish
Cover photo of Lucy Giarruputo by Petra Mackay

A catalogue record for this book
is available from the British Library

ISBN: 978-0-00-733262-5

Contents

Introduction

Dear Reader,

It's fourteen years since I wrote my first book on parenting. My life has been greatly affected by people's responses to *The Secret of Happy Children* over those years. Whenever Shaaron and I travel around the world, it is like meeting friends who already know us. The confidence that people put in us makes us both proud and anxious. What inspires us is the fact that people everywhere care SO much about their kids.

Parenthood is deep water. It can occasionally make you happier than anything else in your life, but you will also sometimes feel like your heart is being kicked around on the footpath! Don't let anyone tell you that it is simple.

Today there are dozens of parenting books on the shelves. So logical and cheerful! Full of breezy advice and long tidy lists of what to do. Four steps to confident kids! Who are they kidding?

On the other hand, something has to be done – since many parents are desperate for answers. So, where does this second book fit in? It is a deeper book than the first one. It is also more specific, since it is based on work with thousands more parents who have told us what works. The ideas of softlove and firmlove, which you'll learn about in this book, are powerful tools that can turn family life around. They address the real aims of parenthood – to produce young adults with warm hearts and lots of backbone.

There are also two big challenges for mothers and fathers embedded in this book:

- to give up violence and fear-based methods of discipline
- to really raise your own children, and not leave this job to others.

It's clear that raising kids sends you on an inner journey of self- discovery. This is certainly worthwhile. So – no quick answers in this book. Instead, some powerful ideas to help you find 'your own right way'.

Much love to your family from ours,

Steve Biddulph

PS The wombats have grown up and left home!

Experts can be a hazard to your family's health.
Luckily, this is a non-expert book!
Please take it for what it is – friendly suggestions,
and support for your own good sense.

In your heart,
YOU know what's right
for you and your children.

1

Making tomorrow's people

Imagine this. You are sitting on the front porch. In front of you are gardens and a leafy street – there is no sound but the singing of birds. You are old, but still tanned and fit, and wearing warm, soft clothes.

A sleek and almost silent vehicle rolls up. Its doors click open, and some young adults step out. They are your grown-up children!

They give you big hugs. They are full of energy, and happy to see you. They sit down and tell you their latest adventures, new achievements and news of their families. You bring out food and drinks, and talk over many things. Eventually, it's time for them to leave.

You go inside and put on a warm sweater.

For a long time you sit by the window, remembering back to when they were children. You feel very proud of how they have turned out, of what you have given the world.

Seeing your kids as a gift

If you were to believe the media, you'd think that kids are nothing but one big problem – a behaviour problem, a childcare problem, a health problem.

This is a terrible con, because the truth is … kids are a beautiful gift. Deep down we really know this, but sometimes we forget. The one in five couples who have fertility problems know what a gift children are. So do the parents whose children battle with illness or disability. When our children are endangered, we suddenly realize that they matter so much, and that other things matter so little.

There *are* real challenges in raising kids. In this book we'll tackle many of these. But you should start by reminding yourself what a fantastic thing to have in your life – the shaping of a new life, the launching of a wonderful human being into the future. You will give and receive. Your life will be greatly enriched by the love and adoration you can receive from your children, who approach everything with freshness, intensity and trust.

We are now raising *twenty-first-century children*, and are actually doing quite well – creating a kind of young person who is light years ahead of the young adults of thirty years ago. (Compare yourself at fifteen, say, with what fifteen-year-olds are like now!)

Raising kids is an ancient craft. To do it well you have to root out your hidden inner resources, as well as drawing on many outer supports. You adopt a kind of 'finding the way as you go' attitude – being willing to make mistakes and learn from them without hassling yourself unduly. That willingness to learn is probably what made you pick up this book.

You love your kids, you want to do your very best and you are willing to learn. You have all the ingredients to be a fine parent!

Two kinds of love

We love our kids. But love is more than just a warm feeling – it involves some skill. Family therapists recognize that parents need to have two core qualities. I call these *softlove* and *firmlove*. Both these kinds of love have to be activated in sufficient quantities in a parent's make-up, so that children receive the right ingredients to thrive. They are both available in *you*, but you may need some help to awaken them.

WHAT IS SOFTLOVE?

Softlove is the ability to be relaxed, warm and affectionate. It is the ability to stop your brain racing around, to trust your instincts and to fend off the many pressures put on you from outside so that you can *be there* for your child. When you can relax and be yourself, your loving-ness will just naturally arise.

You don't have to force softlove, but you *do* have to give it space to grow. Not everyone was raised with softlove, and so sometimes we find it hard to activate. If you had rather distant or aloof parents, then you may feel tense or uneasy, rather than relaxed and loving, when you are around babies or toddlers. As men and women rediscover softlove, then many things will change for the better. Chapter 2 tells you how this is done.

WHAT IS FIRMLOVE?

Firmlove is the ability to be kind but firm with kids – to make clear rules and back them up, without getting angry, without being weak and giving in. It's the quality people speak of when they say, 'That person has backbone.'

Many people are confused about love because they think it is always warm and gooey. For instance, a father lends large amounts of money to his teenage daughter who 'forgets' to pay him back. This isn't love – it's just 'sogginess'. Firmlove means saying, 'Of course I love you. And you owe me £30. So no more loans till you pay me back!'

Firmlove is strength with a loving intention, as opposed to being cold and hard. Good parents are firm with little children often, because they love them. Often this relates to *safety* – 'I love you, and that's why I won't let you run off down the street.' Or *respect for others* – 'In this house people don't hit each other.'

Good parents are willing to be tough with their kids because they know this will help them to have a happier life.

FINDING THE BALANCE

No one gets it right every time. Giving softlove and firmlove to your kids is always a matter of finding your way, finding the balance as you go along. A parent who is kind and firm says things like – 'No, you are not going out in the rain and cold. How about looking for something interesting to do in the kitchen?' They are aware of their child's needs for activity – 'I understand you are bored – I'll help you find something to do.' But they are clear in their decision –'You have to stay indoors when it's wet.'

PROBLEMS ARE YOUR CUE TO ADJUST THE BALANCE

The so-called 'problems' that arise from time to time in every family are just your child's way of letting you know that the balance needs to change. For example, a little girl will get a tummyache because Mum and Dad have been too busy with the new baby. A boy will get into trouble at school to get more attention from his dad.

Sometimes you will have to develop new levels of either softlove or firmlove in yourself – more than you were ever given as a child – in order to help your child. That's why parenting is such a 'stretching' time – it takes you beyond all your previous limitations. This has to be a good thing, but you will need support and encouragement. The chapters coming up will give you lots of this, with many real-life examples to draw on for inspiration.

UNDERSTANDING YOUR LOVING STYLE

Lots of parents have asked for a simple way to measure how they are doing – and how they can improve. This simple questionnaire can help you to understand the two kinds of love, and to make your parenthood a more positive experience. Circle the number that best reflects your answer.

Softlove questions

1. I give my kids lots of hugs. I love to hold them and tell them how great they are.

   Not at all. 1   2   3   4   5 *Very much.*

2. I am a peaceful kind of person. I don't hurry. I can spend hours with my children just enjoying being together.

   Not at all. 1   2   3   4   5 *Very much.*

Now total the two scores above and enter your softlove total here.

SOFTLOVE TOTAL _____

Firmlove questions

1. I can be clear, strong and set rules, and get my children to follow them. The kids know when I mean business and nearly always obey.

   Not at all. 1   2   3   4   5 *Very much.*

2. I am calm and good humoured, so when I am being firm I don't often get really angry. I certainly never lash out at or hit my kids.

   Not at all. 1   2   3   4   5 *Very much.*

6

Now total the two scores above and enter your firmlove total here.

FIRMLOVE TOTAL _____

Now, enter your scores on the graph below.

FIRMLOVE SCORE

1. Put a cross where your *firmlove* score goes on this line.

2. Put a cross where your *soft-love* score goes on this line.

SOFTLOVE SCORE

3. Draw lines across and down from your two scores and mark where they meet. This is your loving style result.

4. Look on the following page for an explanation of your result.

READING YOUR SCORES

Roger is a strong, no-nonsense type of person who is well-organized. Maybe deep down he cares, but finds it hard to show this. So he is aloof and remote, and his kids may feel they are never quite good enough. He is often too busy to spend time with them. (Recently, though, he is starting to change his ways.)

Penny is warm and very loving. She is also quite clear about discipline on the things that matter. Her kids know they have to follow certain guidelines and take on responsibilities. But they also feel safe and cared about. Everyone in this family has lots of fun, hugs and laughter.

Firm but cold
Work on softlove skills described in chapter 2.

Warm and strong
Great!

10
9
8
7
6
5

0   1   2   3   4   6   7   8   9   10

Cold and not very strong
Work through chapters 2 and 3. Seek help from a caring counsellor if you feel concerned about your parenting.

4
3
2
1
0

Loving but not very firm
Work on firmlove skills described in chapter 3.

Agnes is very tense and distant. She may let her children get away with murder, and then loses it completely and lashes out at them. Then she feels sorry and goes back to being permissive again. (With the help of friends and a counsellor she is learning to relax and love herself so she can love her children.)

Cheryl loves her kids and spends lots of time with them. In fact, she has no time for herself. The children walk all over her, and are very demanding. Cheryl is terribly tired from trying so hard, and yet can't seem to gain control. (She has started going to a parents' support group and is getting some hints on firmlove.)

> The author wishes to apologize to any Agneses, Pennys, Rogers or Cheryls who feel that this is not them at all! No resemblance to any persons living, dead or otherwise is intended.

Softlove

Making contact with your child

All parents love their children.

The big question is: 'Will my love get through?'

It's dusk, and the bush around the lake is silent, apart from a distant lonely bird call. In a cottage by the water, a man and a woman are making love. They begin slowly, taking their time, enjoying the anticipation and the gradual falling away of tensions and cares. They are getting to know each other afresh, though they have been partners for many years now. After a time, the energy and passion begins to rise, her laughter mingles with his urgency, and soon they are both crying out in pleasure. Afterwards, there is a quiet resting and sleepy settling-together of warm bodies. Later, inside the woman's body, as they both sleep, a sperm finds its way to the waiting, moon-like ovum, and a child's life begins.

Loving the life inside you

How did you get to be a parent? You got pregnant – obviously!

Did you want to get pregnant? Who knows? Your body certainly wanted to. To your conscious mind, though, becoming pregnant can be a shock. Even the most highly planned pregnancy (not to mention the most totally 'accidental') brings this feeling. As you hold that little plastic test stick, you think 'Oh my!' The rollercoaster ride has begun!

Being pregnant confronts you with a choice. You can reach out with love to this new life inside you, or you can pull back in fear and caution. As your child grows inside you, is born and grows up, you will again and again have the choice to harden your heart and pull back, or to soften your heart and respond with the quality we call softlove.

Softlove – the capacity for tenderness, generosity and warmth – dwells inside every single person.

The softlove inside you may be strong like a fierce flame or it may stay like a tiny glowing spark, unnoticed, waiting to be kindled. Every new mother or father has this spark inside them. Researchers have found that when fathers are present at the birth, or get involved in the early care of babies, they become 'engrossed' in the child – deeply interested and deeply satisfied – wanting to spend more of their time around the baby, and wanting to become skilled in the baby's care. This is true whether or not the baby is their own biological child. The key is being there early.

A mother's body, if she is able to sleep alongside her baby from the very first, and especially if she is helped to breastfeed, releases powerful hormones called prolactins which actually make her want to mother. These hormones relax her and slow her down, giving her deep pleasure in being with her little ones. They prime her body for awareness and vigilance around babies. Whenever you feel clucky, drawn to anything small and furry, this is prolactin at work.

A note about breastfeeding. The evidence grows continually that breastfeeding provides nutrients and antibodies which make it far superior to artificial milk. Sometimes a mother has to bottle-feed through medical necessity, in which case it is important for her to bare her skin for the baby to feel while feeding. She should relax and make eye contact with her baby, and generally allow feed time to be a time of intimacy. We believe that breastfeeding is an art – mothers sometimes need understanding help to breastfeed successfully, and there are simple tips that can make all the difference. We recommend contacting the National Childbirth Trust or National Breastfeeding Alliance. They can provide wonderful individual help in most parts of Britain.

So the loving feelings are inbuilt and waiting to be awakened. Sometimes this happens easily and smoothly. Sometimes it needs help.

When you were a child, did you learn how to love? If you didn't receive much love in your own childhood and babyhood, this can be one of the biggest barriers to letting your love flow – it may be that you didn't 'learn to love'. But it's never too late.

Our parents' generation cared about their children – but they didn't always show it, or say it very often. Many of today's parents were not raised with affection as babies and toddlers. In the 'icy 1950s', when medicine ruled birth and babyhood, it was considered 'spoiling' to be kind to a child. Parents were instructed to leave their babies to cry, or were afraid to feed them unless the clock said they could, or worried they would corrupt their children by cuddling them. Even today some authors and paediatricians advise letting babies cry out their distress alone in their room. What a disaster!

Jean Liedloff, in an article in *Mothering* magazine, concludes there are two basic feelings that all human beings need. These are to feel *welcome*, and to feel *worthy*. In the 1950s and 1960s, parents were often quite good at the mechanical side of parenting – feeding and clothing us and keeping us well. This was a pretty good start. But they often had trouble being warm or close, and in those days shame and blame were a big part of the discipline style. One could well grow up feeling unwelcome, and unworthy to boot!

One man explained to us that in his teens and twenties he felt a strong need to be around older, kinder people, just to bathe in the feeling of being welcomed in, given a smile, being asked about his day. Gradually, through doing this, he filled in the gaps in his feelings of welcome. After a time, he also knew that people liked his company, asked his opinion, told him their problems – and that made him feel worthy. In the end he became a psychologist!

An elderly friend told us that when she was a girl she used to feel very lonely and unloved. At midnight, when others were asleep, she would turn on the radio. The announcer on the late programme had a deep, friendly voice. She would stay awake to hear him wish everyone 'Goodnight and God bless.' Then she felt cared about and comforted, and slept soundly.

There were some plusses about childhood in 'the old days'. People tended to have lots of babies and lived close to their relatives, so older children, nieces, nephews, aunties and grandmas all helped with the babies. You got lots of practice at being a parent before you became one. (Today a quarter of new parents have never even *held* a baby until the day they first hold their own. No wonder they are terrified.)

To avoid parenthood becoming a big struggle you must get extra help for yourself – learning to receive love, so you can love your baby well. This begins very early. Research has found that the presence of a support person at the birth – someone who loves and cares about the mother – dramatically reduces the incidence of Caesareans, and of epidurals (and therefore forceps deliveries). Emotional care – in this case, of the mother – has real physical consequences.

Love is a real, tangible substance, and things go better when there is more love around. Once your baby is born, the best love people can give you is often practical: massage (for you), special meals, time and care, as well as help to protect your privacy. All of these kinds of loving can help to awaken your own loving capacities.

In short, if you had a secure and loving childhood, then things are likely to go well with your kids. But even if you didn't – and many of us didn't – then you can still turn things around for yourself and your children.

HEALING A MOTHER HELPS A SON

Esme, thirty-eight, had a difficult relationship with her teenage son. In fact, he was very depressed and possibly suicidal. We talked about how she and he got along. It was clear that almost every conversation they had involved her criticizing him. On the inside she cared, but on the outside she was cool and stiff, very unhappy in herself. As she felt safer with me, Esme confided that she rarely (if ever) hugged her son or touched him in an affectionate way. The very idea of touching him made her uncomfortable.

Emotional coolness on a mother's part is known to be a danger sign for suicide in teenage boys, especially if the father is also ineffectual or distant. So we made closeness our first goal. With encouragement, Esme began to reach out more. She practised casually putting a hand on her son's shoulder as she gave him his dinner, and giving him small compliments on his hair or clothes. After a week or two she moved up to giving him a brief hug when he left for school.

Esme found it hard to do these things, but she persisted. Then, one day in a self-development course she was attending, she was listening to someone in the group talking about their painful childhood. Suddenly she found she was shaking and shivering, and soon she was sobbing out loud. She was remembering being sexually assaulted by her father when she was about four. (Fortunately, her mother had left her father shortly after that.)

Esme had not so much forgotten these incidents, but had played down their importance to herself. Here was the reason why she found touch and affection difficult.

Through talking little by little in the group about her experiences, Esme learned to let others care for her, and she rapidly became a more outgoing person. All these qualities had been latent inside her, but were hidden by the fear of a little four-year-old girl whose trust had been betrayed. So helping her son turned into helping herself, too.

The power of touch When you read the story of Esme and her son, did it surprise you that touch and affection could make the difference between a youngster wanting to live and wanting to die? Can touch really be that important?

On the surface, one wouldn't think that teenagers would be so concerned about their parents' affection. But a teenager was once a baby. And if they were not cuddled and stroked back then, it was a serious matter indeed.

Starved of affection, a little baby can literally die of loneliness. When a premature baby is stroked, growth hormones are produced. It's as if a baby decides life is worth living. When we receive loving touch our immune system fires up and resists infection much more readily. Haemoglobin (iron-carrying) levels in the blood increase dramatically.

Touch is an 'essential vitamin' for all mammals. When babies are born prematurely, they are often kept in incubators for many weeks. It has been recently discovered that if these babies are regularly stroked by their mother (or another loving person) reaching into the incubator and caressing their little bodies gently, they will gain weight 75 per cent faster than other babies who are not given this stroking. They are discharged weeks earlier, and save the hospital thousands of pounds.

FIND AS MANY WAYS TO TOUCH AS YOU CAN

There are many ways to show affection to small children – massage, stroking, patting, tickling, caressing, carrying, rocking, cuddling, brushing their hair, holding hands, giving rides, swinging, jiggling. Each conveys a different version of the same message – you are loved, you are welcome, you are worthy.

Sometimes older children go through a non-touch phase where they are establishing some independence. An experienced mother of teenagers told us that you still have to 'keep your arms open', because the time will come when they want to be hugged again.

Early problems and deprivations can often be healed later by gradually building up affection, as a child learns to trust. With sufficient time and care, fostered and adopted babies can overcome a difficult beginning. I have often seen and worked with adults who are healing babyhood neglect, and doing it successfully. But how much better to get it right the first time.

As kids get older, there are even more ways to make our love known to them. The most obvious way is with words. We shape their personality – by saying, 'You are beautiful, you are lots of fun, you are good to be around.' Kids become what we tell them they are.

The power of praise

Children need two kinds of telling. One kind is *unconditional* praise – this means that we let them know 'I love you because you are you.' They don't have to earn this love, and they can't ever lose it. Imagine how good this feels – to be unconditionally loved, just because you exist.

The second kind is *conditional* praise. This means that we tell them, 'I appreciate your actions.' For instance, we might say, 'I like the way you entertained your baby sister when the phone rang', or 'I really like your drawings', or 'You sing beautifully', and so on.

It's OK to tell kids what you don't like as well – as long as you don't call them names. 'You didn't pick up your clothes very well – I can still see eight T-shirts and 17 socks on the floor' is fine. 'You lazy little sod' is not so good.

17

Sometimes parents have to learn to *see* the positives before they can point them out. The power of our attention is a very powerful influence on our children. One of our teachers, Ken Mellor, puts it this way: 'What you focus on with kids is what you get.' Some families focus on illness, for example, and always have sick kids. Some focus on complaining (while trying to make everyone happy), and always have grumpy kids. If you look for negatives and always point these out (which some fathers are especially prone to doing), then the negatives will increase. If you let your children know that you notice when they act well, and comment on what they do that is great, then they will act great more of the time!

Quality of the week

Here is an exercise to try.
1. Choose the three qualities you most want your child to have (it could be anything – kindness to others, patience, gentleness, perseverance, cooperation, independence, creativity).
2. Take one of these qualities as your goal for this week.
3. Take note of every time they show this quality. Comment sometimes; other times just simply notice. Make no negative comments at all. By the end of the week, you can be sure this quality will be on the increase. Then move on to another. You can also let your child choose a quality, and notice it together through the week. Point out only when they *do* show the quality.

Time There is one essential ingredient for softlove, and that is being there; or, in other words, having time. However much you *tell* your children you love them, if you are not around enough, then your words will be a lie. With kids it's what you *do*, not what you say, that counts.

OK KIDS- IT'S QUALITY TIME!

Lots of fathers today leave for work at 7.30 a.m. and return at 7.30 p.m. or later. These fathers are not likely to be successful as parents or, if they are, will only be so by making superhuman efforts on holidays and at the weekend. It isn't always their fault – the workplace is not yet a parent-friendly place. In the Stone Age, parents would often have to face a tiger or woolly mammoth to save their children. In the computer age, we might have to tell our boss to get stuffed! – equally dangerous.

It's not just dads – lots of mothers too are being conned by the comforting but largely false concept of 'quality time'. You can't have quality time with children 'to order', by schedule, on the dot. Relationships are a delicate business. If a woman has a husband who suddenly puts down the newspaper or turns off the TV at 10.30 at night, and gets all amorous after ignoring her all evening, she'll know the feeling that kids get when a parent lobs in for 'quality time'!

Certainly it's important to have special times. One easy and very powerful step to take is to sit down for a meal together each day, and switch off the TV or radio. It can be dinner, or even breakfast. Too few families eat together, yet it can be one perfect way to reconnect.

To a large degree, kids decide what they are worth based on what they are worth to you, and based on your enjoyment of their company. Imagine how good it feels to a baby or toddler to know that you value them more highly than almost anything else. As babies and toddlers, they *should* feel this way – not that they are 'the boss' but that their needs really count. This need reduces as they get older, but is still operating well into their teens.

Increasing your capacity for love

What is the quickest way to increase the love and positivity available in your family? You can start by learning a simple skill which all loving people have, often without knowing it. This is the knack of *living in 'present time'*.

Present time is where children live. To them, the future is impossibly far off. Kids live for today!

You were like this once. Can you remember when you were little, and a day seemed like a really long time? When six weeks off school at the start of the summer seemed like for ever?

An adult who can live in the now (at least some of the time) will be an instant hit with children. Old people sometimes have this ability because they've stopped rushing. Most parents (the people who most need to be) are hardly ever in present time. (As a young parent, I was a bad case of this. Whenever I was with my children, my mind would be somewhere else. My toddler son would give me a whack to bring me back to attention.)

Many people seem to have lost the knack of just being – especially if they live in cities, away from the rhythms of nature. Or, worse still, they think they are 'wasting time' or 'not achieving' if a day just drifts by. Yet, if you want to get through to your kids, whether to show them your love or to give them effective discipline, then you have to get yourself back into present time. Here is how to do just that.

GETTING YOUR BRAIN TO COME HOME

Most of the trouble we have in life comes from having a brain. Not just any brain, but a human brain – horribly prone to worries and abstractions which no dog, cat or budgie would ever waste a second on. (A mother once commented at one of my seminars, 'I worry if my children will ever get a job.' I asked how old her kids were and she said, 'Oh, I don't have kids yet!' She'd come along to my talk as a preparation for parenthood! Half of me thought, 'Great!', and half of me thought, 'This gal should be tenpin bowling!')

Our brain can make us miserable because it is always racing off out of control. So we miss out on what is happening right in front of us. There are three ways your brain 'races off'.

1. **Dragging around in the past.** Recalling the past can be very pleasant, but mostly people go into the past to rehash old regrets (what they missed out on), old guilts (what they shouldn't have done but did!) and old resentments (what others didn't do but should have).

   Going over the past, without changing any of it or having any new thoughts, is often a complete waste of time. Yet it probably occupies half of all human mental activity!

2. **Racing ahead to the future.** The future can also be a wonderful place to dream about, but most people just worry about what can go wrong. They use the future to practise 'worst-case scenarios' (a beautiful phrase!). Rent the video *Parenthood*, and watch for the baseball scene for a brilliant example of this.

MY PARENTS WERE PERFECT— I'VE NOTHING TO TELL MY THERAPIST!

MUM! IT'S A WORST CASE SCENARIO!

The trouble with fearing the worst is that it either paralyses you, or else you react to things in an exaggerated way. You overlook the positive because it doesn't fit your plan of disaster. You miss the beauty of the roses because you are imagining yourself catching tetanus from the thorns.

3. **Wishing you were somewhere else** (or thinking you should be). Lots of people make themselves miserable by wishing they had made the other decision – taken that job, done that course, married the other guy or girl, lived in that other town, not had this baby. They are in one place, but hanker for another. Everyone does this at times, but sensible people use the energy to make changes, plan a holiday, or organize the future to more resemble the dreams they have. Others, though, just hanker. If only . . . aah, then I would be happy.

While we are busy racing off in our minds, we are making ourselves miserable, and we are missing out on our children.

In case you hadn't noticed by now, many of the best times in life just happen. Happiness often doesn't come according to plan. (Sometimes it does – the planned holiday or outing, a family occasion, a well-deserved trip to a restaurant or the movies.) But for every planned happiness there are ten accidental ones that will only happen if you allow them to – if you have enough time to appreciate them. Happiness is like a butterfly, waiting for you to stop still so it can land on your shoulder.

Happiness, like a child, dwells in the present

Magic moments

Life delivers us pearls of happiness when we least expect them. (Biscuit ads and new car commercials on TV try to capture these moments.)

You know the kind of thing – you're in a paddock or park with your children trying to fly a kite. It's cloudy. First of all the kite won't fly, then suddenly – it's up! The kids are running towards you with the kite behind. An eagle soars overhead. The sun is out suddenly and shining through their hair like golden haloes. Everything goes into slow motion, and are those violins you hear? Your partner smiles at you adoringly and you are suddenly and absolutely 'blissed out'. You wouldn't be anywhere else on earth!

Children store up these moments in their memory banks. At quiet times, or on long car trips, your kids will play 'Remember when . . . ?', recalling in detail the good times they had at that place and this. It builds their sense of belonging and their optimism for the future. Can you remember the really magical moments in your own childhood? I can remember a day at a football match with my dad, being kept warm inside his long overcoat. I can remember being held by my mother on the toilet when I was a toddler. She sat on the laundry basket opposite me, and I leaned on to her lap. Perhaps she was worried I would fall in. Whatever the reason, it felt nice. I remember making it last!

HAPPY ENDINGS – EVERY DAY!

One family we know has a five-year-old son and a two-year-old daughter. Each night, when they go to bed, these kids have a special ritual. Instead of reading a story, their mum or dad recounts the events of the day.

At the end of this story, they tell their child what was the very best part of the day for them. Then they ask their child, 'What was the best part of your day?' and listen carefully to what they have to say. Then they kiss goodnight.

It's a beautiful way to end the day, and a very powerful programming of energy towards the positive.

MADNESS RUNS IN FAMILIES

Family life these days often resembles organized madness. Parents rise before 6.00 a.m., gulp food, rush children to breakfast club, then to school, which takes them to after-school club. They pick them up after work, go home, cook tea, have 'quality time' (ho, ho!), do housework or office work brought home, and then collapse asleep after midnight.

Families today often own houses which require both adults working for thirty years to pay off. Some parents spend a quarter of their waking time sitting in a vehicle. Fathers work back at nights to pay private-school fees for children who hate school anyway, and have low self-esteem and drug problems because their fathers are never home. Marriages collapse from neglect and fatigue, but both partners blame 'communication problems'. Both partners get more quality communication with the tea lady! The British family seems to be dying of stress.

Being 'grounded' – a technique for calming down

Grounding is a powerful and simple way of getting your mind to settle down and be focused in the here and now. You can do grounding anywhere – driving a car, doing the dishes, walking down the corridor, making love. Here is how it is done.

Why not try this right now, as you read. Start by noticing your own body's 'inside sensations' – how your muscles feel, how your insides feel. Just notice these inner sensations, however slight. Focus on the inner sensations in your body, however vague they might be. Then start to notice what you are touching – your hands on this book (are your shoulders relaxed?), the chair pressing your back, the feel of your clothes on your skin. Just notice and intensify the sensations that are already there.

After a time, shift your focus to the outside. Look around you, smell and listen to what is around you. Become intensely aware of your surroundings. Literally 'come to your senses'.

You will notice the three distinct layers of experience: your *insides* (the sensations inside your body) – are you energetic, tired, relaxed, do you need to shift your position?; your *edges* – what you are touching, your hands on this book, the air on your face; and your *environment* – what is going on around you, what sounds, what colours, what action is around you?

As you notice these three zones of awareness without expecting or judging anything, you will become aware of several effects.

Your mind will slow down.

You will intensify the present moment – the beauty of it, the richness of it.

Your body signals come through more strongly, telling you there is something that needs to be done – stretch your legs, go for a pee, get something to eat! And so on.

At times, we are all troubled by an overactive mind. The best way to calm your mind is to give it something to attend to, something that is real and present. If you are driving a car, notice the feel of the steering wheel; if you are stacking the dishwasher, the feel of the dishes; if you are sitting with your child, the touch and temperature of their body against yours.

Unlike relaxation, grounding can be done anywhere in a matter of seconds. Using grounding takes practice and mindfulness, but it is as natural as breathing. Do it, and it will be totally reliable in improving your state of mind. Little children are usually already grounded. People who are very natural, rhythmic and down to earth are grounded and you can learn to be the same by just being around them. As you learn to be grounded more of the time, you will be less interested in being any other way. You will notice when you are getting too speedy or agitated, or depressed and stuck in your thoughts. You will be able to bring yourself smoothly back to the pleasures of the here and now.

You can't give love if you don't have a clear sense of self. And a sense of self only comes when you give yourself space to be. Every day, you must keep some time just for yourself.

Self time – what every parent needs

Some people get up early, or stay up late when everyone else has gone to bed, to get this time. Others make a deal with their partner to provide some self time for each other.

Self time is even more important than couple time, because you cannot connect with your partner until you have re-established a sense of self. Once you are happy in yourself, you will feel like being close to another person, but not usually until then.

Self time doesn't mean doing housework, though sometimes a big cleanup while the kids are minded can be very satisfying. It could mean time with friends. Watching TV doesn't do it well – you lose yourself rather than find yourself. Writing works very well – letters or a journal. Praying or meditation are good if you have a spiritual dimension in your life. Reading is pretty good. Lie in the bath with a glass of wine and a magazine! Head off to the bush, go into the garden, walk the dog. Everyone has their preferred way of having self time. The important thing is to do it and to schedule it regularly.

THE TREE OF (FAMILY) LIFE

You grow a family like you grow a tree. The roots are your own childhood and how you care for yourself. The trunk is your marriage or partnership, and your commitment to your kids. The branches are your actions based on choices you make every day. Your kids are the flowers and the fruit.

We live in as natural a way as possible, try to eat clean food, and work to make our world and neighbourhood better and safer places.

We dance around and play music and sing.

I protect my kids from exposure to dangerous people and violent or cheap media.

I hug my kids, and laugh and play with them often.

I work on my relationship and set aside time to get to know my partner. I do this for myself, for my partner and for my children.

We cultivate good friendships. Relationships with grandparents, neighbours, cousins and special friends provide a support network that I can confide in.

I am firm about my kids' behaviour, especially about respect for each other's rights and feelings.

I take steps to control how much my job intrudes on my family and my life.

I really like my children and enjoy spending time with them. They make me feel good (most of the time).

I'd rather be with my kids and be poor than have money but no time to spend with them.

I care for myself, and have time just to be me.

People were kind to me when I was young and I enjoy passing that on to the children of today.

OR I had a tough time as a kid, so I know it's important to 'water and feed the roots'. This will help me to do good things and to get good things and good care for myself.

Once, long ago, I worked in a high school with drop-out children. One day during recess time, a group of my twelve-year-olds disappeared behind a huge stack of damaged furniture and I could hear giggles and shuffling sounds from deep in the heap. I suspected 'evil-doing' and crawled in to investigate. To my embarrassment, they were sharing their lunches and drinks in a kind of cubby house! They invited me to join them, but I just grinned and crawled ashamedly outside to the noisy world. I'd forgotten these were really just children, needing to play.

Perhaps the most serious and insidious harm that has been done to children in the last twenty years has been caused by the way we have taken away their childhood. There are several ways that this happens.

1. **A media bombardment** Horror, fear, grief and pain are compressed daily into our media news and our entertainment. TV has a little screen, so it has to have a big shock to hold our attention. The media blasts the same messages at toddlers as it does at sixty-year-olds. We heap our children with needless negativity which is not relevant to their lives and which they are in no way equipped to deal with.

2. **An overprogrammed life** Many families I know of spend evenings and weekends shuffling children to a range of sports, music, culture and supplementary learning venues. When all these 'extras' are combined with homework pressures, the average child has very little time just to be a child. We have the most overscheduled generation that ever existed. A solution to this might be a simple rule – one child, one activity.

3. **A competitive neurosis** Partly fuelling the second point is the feeling, easily caught by children, that life is a desperate race. So school takes on an anxious, performance-laden aura, even

from kindergarten. Instead of playing around, children join a competitive, organized, often expensive sport. Seven-year-olds are comparing their scores, worrying about their performances, praying they will make the team. This is madness.

4. **Overworked parents** Since we are so busy providing all these goodies, we have little time or energy to make contact. We become tense, snappy, and poor confidantes to our children. Feeling more guilty, we provide more possessions and experiences, and then have to work harder still to pay for them.

5. **An unsafe world** Whereas once children roamed the neighbourhoods and countryside of 1950s Britain, barely seen from breakfast till dinner, we now have to guard them carefully and protect them from traffic, strangers and crime.

We need a re-greening of childhood – a conservationist approach. We have to conserve the rare, natural and wild part of our children. This is an active process – cutting out and fencing off needless pressures and invasions. We have to 'de-pollute' our children's lives.

SOME POSSIBLE CLUES

- Have lots of time, space and materials for simple play. Plastic toys are cheap and clean, but mud and scrap paper, clay and water are the best toys. They give absolutely free rein to the child's own inclinations and imagination.

- Create healthy boredom – kids used to being entertained by computer screens, videos or schedules of 'educational' activity will take a little while to switch over to self-initiated play. You may have to resist 'I'm bored' for a time until they begin self-starting.

- Play is valuable in itself. Psychologists are discovering that this is the way children make sense of their world, act out concerns, overcome fears and learn to relate to others. Play is the source of all creativity and inventiveness. The great musicians, scientists, lovers, artists, and

even managers, are the ones who have preserved the ability to play
with their ideas and their work.

- You can play too – adults in crisis or transition often find healing in
  creativity, music, natural places, movement and the outdoors.

- Stop watching the evening news. Don't have a TV set running in
  the house – choose programmes and watch them, then turn the TV
  off. Give kids an hour a day and let them select what they will
  watch.

- Consider your whole lifestyle in this question. Do you really like
  where you live, how you live and the work that you do? Are there
  alternatives that would make your life more joyful, simpler, and yet
  still stimulating and rich? Perhaps we are living at a time when the
  whole world needs to 'wind down'. Children give you a good reason
  to do this.

Sometimes the arrival of babies in our lives kicks us into a frenzy of
overactivity – renovating, working overtime to save for school fees, trying to provide what we think they need ... when all the time what they
really need is us!

My work with families in distress has given me an extra spur to not
wasting my life with busyness – in one simple and trenchant way. Sometimes children die – and if we have missed out on the present while
working for the future, then we will feel very bad indeed.

The best thing you can do for your children is enjoy them.

3

Firmlove

The secret
of well-behaved children

It's a sign of the times that people are even using the word 'discipline' again. For those of us who came through the 1960s, this is an amazing turnaround. For about twenty years, the only place you heard of discipline was in ads for Madame Lash's House of Domination (whatever that was). But sure enough, as you leaf through family magazines and scan the bookshelves, discipline is back on the agenda. And not a moment too soon. When most modern house plans include a room called a parents' retreat, then it's clearly time to act. Let's reclaim the house!

Why discipline? Uh-oh! You have just spotted them coming up the drive. Your best friend with her child – the toddler from hell. The kid who puts jam on your sofa, writes on the curtains and frightens pit bull terriers. Should you answer the door? Is there time to hide?

Discipline is a funny thing – you notice it most when it isn't there. Everyone knows someone with a completely out-of-control child and many of us have one of our own! Getting cooperation is a problem at times for almost every parent. Most British parents today are confused about discipline.

A small number of parents, on the other hand, seem to have it all sorted out. What is their secret? These parents call their toddler to 'come along now' and the toddler actually comes! You visit their house and your mouth hangs open. Their ten-year-old cooks tea for the family. Their teenagers phone to say they'll be home early. And these kids are not frightened mice – they're happy, optimistic and relaxed. How do these parents do it?

We all long to have well-disciplined kids for one simple reason – it makes life go more smoothly. Giving in to kids doesn't make life easier. Parents who are reluctant to set boundaries find that their kids just get worse. Without clear rules, you and your child may spend the whole day hassling and everyone feels bad at the end of it. Whereas if you have a discipline method that works quickly, problems are soon solved and you can get on with being happy.

There is more to it though. We don't discipline kids just for our own sakes – just to have 'law and order'. After all, if you want an orderly life, you don't have kids. The real purpose of discipline is to teach children to operate happily and easily in the world.

Without some parental firmness, children don't develop inner controls, and just keep on acting like two-year-olds, even when they are five, fifteen, twenty-five. Without inner discipline, a child's life is a mess. Parents who let children do as they like will severely disable them for living in the real world. These kids may end up unhappy, unemployed, unmarried, lonely, angry, and perhaps even in jail. A child who has been taught good self-discipline, on the other hand, learns how to negotiate the world and stay out of trouble, and so is really free.

Discipline is about getting along with yourself and with other people. After love, there is nothing more important you can give them than discipline. But not the kind of discipline that has often been implied by that word.

The approach to discipline we recommend is called *firmlove* – it is intervening out of love for the child. A parent using firmlove says, 'I love you, and that's why I will stop you behaving like this.' They combine love and firmness. They never hit, they never harm, they never blame. But they *are* firm.

'Stand and think' and 'dealing'

By now, you may be asking: 'What is this miraculous method of getting cooperation?' It's a good time to explain. Firmlove rests on two main techniques – the first is called '*stand and think*' and the second is called '*dealing*'. These methods are used from toddlerhood onwards, modified and developed as your child grows, and adaptable into adolescence and adulthood. In fact, the ability to 'stand and think' and 'deal' will become inner resources throughout your child's adult life, helping them to be mature, reflective and wise in all their dealings.

Let's find out how it's done.

LUCY MEETS HER MATCH

Twenty-month-old Lucy is playing with the power cords at the back of the stereo. She isn't doing this quietly or sneakily – she is in full view of her mother and father, who are deep in conversation. Her mother sees her and calls out, 'Lucy, hands off those power points. Come away and play with your toys.'

Lucy doesn't even budge. Her mother stands up and goes over to her – 'Lucy, hands off the power points, come over here.' Lucy looks up and gives the famous 'What are you going to do about it?' look. Her mother gives it one more try – 'Come away from the power points!' Lucy turns back to rewiring the stereo, muttering 'No, No, No!' under her breath.

Up until today, Lucy has never done anything this naughty. She has always been able to be diverted or negotiated away from trouble. Today, though, is her first real discipline experience. She is inviting her parents to struggle with her because this is what she needs.

It's time for action. Lucy's mother moves in briskly, grabs Lucy around the waist from behind with both hands, lifts her clear and takes her to the other side of the room where there is a free corner (every lounge should have a free corner). Lucy does not welcome this attention. She screams, yells, hits out and flails (which is why her Mum is holding her from behind!). Her mum continues to hold her firmly, safely, and tells her, 'When you are ready to calm down, you can come out.'

Lucy goes through many 'moves' that may be familiar to you – spitting, trying to bite, attempting to vomit her dinner up. Other children may hold their breath, call you names, and so on. Lucy has never been smacked and is not at all afraid. In fact, she is furious. How dare anyone interfere with her impulses! She looks to her father, who is standing back across the room. 'Daddy, helpa me!' Her father moves in and helps to hold her. He repeats what her mother has been telling her, in a calm, reassuring tone: 'You must stay away from power cords Lucy.' After what seems like ten minutes, but is actually about one minute, Lucy stops fighting and quietens down. Her mother has been saying to her softly the whole time, 'When you are ready to calm down, you can come out.' She now asks Lucy straight out, 'Now, are you going to stay away from the powerpoints?' 'Yeth!' she says.

Both parents stand back. 'Good girl,' they say, and watch to see what she will do. Lucy looks at the power points. She looks at her parents. She looks at her toys on the other side of the room. Then she heads over to the toys. And her mum and dad give a big sigh of relief and sit back down. In the weeks that follow, Lucy will try 'poking in the power cords' once more, and stop when spoken to.

She will be in and out of the 'thinking spot' many times before she is five years old – for all kinds of reasons. By the age of two-and-a-half she will usually go there when told to, and stand quietly and think over what she needs to learn. By five, she will have learned to think, to consider her actions, to account for the feelings of others, and still be a happy, spontaneous and easy-going child.

No hurt, no blame, no fear

For little Lucy, getting carried off to 'stand and think' was a surprise, but only her pride was dented – and only for a matter of minutes. With little children, we sometimes have to be physical, although always safe, and never scary. By carrying a screaming toddler away from a supermarket when they want to stay, restraining them from pouring soft drink into a sleeping dog's ears, breaking up a melee at the playgroup – we have to physically let them know 'that's not on!' With a toddler, we have to match words with actions. Move calmly without hurting (even when you are angry). In fact it's best to act early, long before you lose your cool. If you feel too stirred up, then forget the dealing, and just put them in their room till you cool down.

Soon you will be able simply to tell your child to go to a chosen spot in the room, to 'stand and think'. They will do so, knowing there is no option, but also knowing that it won't take long and isn't a big issue or a punishment – just the way forward through a problem. The emphasis is on the child finding a solution that is acceptable.

Beyond the old methods

There have been three main approaches to discipline over the past hundred years. Traditionally, people used hitting and hurting to frighten kids into behaving. Later, as hitting fell from favour, parents instead used blame and guilt to shame children into behaving. In recent times, people have used isolation methods such as 'time out'. As we know from sending adults to prison, isolating people often doesn't teach them much. So very little changes.

Firmlove goes beyond any of these, recognizing that discipline is about getting involved and teaching. Discipline is not about punishment. One of the great things about firmlove – using 'stand and think' and learning to 'deal' – is that you will never need to smack or hit your kids. Your children – and perhaps one day all children – can grow up without fearing their parents in any way. Can you imagine how good that would feel?

Firmlove means confronting children, certainly, and letting them handle some discomfort, but never inflicting pain. The aim of firmlove is simply to help children find better ways.

Let's look at another instance.

SEAN EATS HIS PEAS

Picture this. After four years of parenthood, Dave and his wife Louise decide it's high time they started to eat out again – with their little boy Sean in tow. They don't see why it shouldn't be possible to go to a nice place (one with tablecloths) and have a quiet meal, even with a child.

Plans are set in motion, and soon they are at the restaurant starting to eat their meal. But young Sean is not happy. Mum and Dad are looking at each other and not at him. He's bored. So he starts to flick his peas. His dad gives him a whispered caution – 'Stop flicking your peas!' But the way he says it sends another message – 'Please, not here, not in front of all these people.' Sean flicks another pea. His dad looks at his mum, who just looks right back. A lot is at stake.

Dave, the dad, gets determined. 'Eat normally, or you'll have to go and stand by the wall,' he says. Sean flicks another pea. Unbelievable! Boys always want their fathers to have backbone and to be true to their word. Dave is true to his – he marches with Sean (gently but firmly, as they say in the textbooks) past forty or so amazed diners, and leaves him in the corner of the restaurant. 'I'll come and talk to you when you look ready to sit and eat sensibly,' he says, and calmly walks back to his table.

Sean is a bit bluffed by all this. Soon his shoulders sag and he looks anxiously back across the room. Dave heads over and asks him, 'Are you ready to deal?' 'Yes.' 'What did you do wrong?' 'Flicked my peas.' 'What are you going to do now?' 'Eat normally.' 'OK. Well done.' And they walk back to the table.

A quiet kind of 'Yaay!' can be heard from tables all around the restaurant. Other parents, who paid babysitters £25 so that they could come out, can be seen taking notes on napkins – 'Are you ready to deal? What did you do? What should you have done?'

Had Sean been a child unused to 'stand and think' it might have been safer to take him out of the restaurant. He might have yelled and squirmed, and it would have been easier for his dad (and other diners) if he did this outside. If you do this with your child, don't leave him. Some firm talking, and the sudden change of environment, usually get Sean to realize that he will be better off settling down. Dave knows that this is a learning moment and that future restaurant meals depend on it.

IS IT NAUGHTINESS OR IS IT JUST ENERGY?

You only have to look at the human body to realize it is made for movement. In his beautiful book, *The Songlines*, Bruce Chatwin reports that Bushmen and women in the Kalahari carry their babies for 4000 kilometres on average before the little ones can walk by themselves.

Our bodies were designed to range over many kilometres each day. So adults or children will feel restless and bored just staying still. Worse still, playing a computer game or watching exciting TV will make kids feel quite twitchy – since these activities create adrenaline with nothing to expend it on. Kids *have* to get outside and get lots of whole-body exercise every day.

Occupational therapist Kerry Anne Brown believes that many later skills like reading, handwriting, posture, and coordination generally, depend on children running, climbing, bouncing, catching and expending huge amounts of energy in the early years of school. These early activities help organize the brain and build muscles to assist in the development of smaller movements like pen-holding later on. Even carrying little babies in slings and backpacks really helps – as do all those rough and tumble games that dads tend to play with little ones on the lounge floor.

A trampoline is a great investment, and any kind of climbing and swinging devices that are safe and well designed are worth their weight in gold.

Parks are also a big plus. Lobby your council to provide plenty of playgrounds in warm, sheltered spots, with shade from the sun and seats for adults. They should be near houses, not off in unsafe areas where young mums feel exposed. They should be well fenced, so you can read a magazine and not worry that your kids can wander off. Good clean toilet facilities would help.

When you are going up the wall, go to a park. I have spent many Saturdays on 'playground crawls' which, with occasional snacks and sandwiches, kept my kids totally satisfied on the cheap!

1. Preparation. Ask yourself, 'What's wrong here? What do I want them to do to fix it?' In other words, have a clear goal before you start.

2. Learning to stand and think is a skill in itself. With a young toddler, it is enough to take them to the spot you have decided on, and then stand back a little. Tell them, 'You have to stay there until you are ready to agree. You can come out when you've calmed down' or, if you are holding them, 'I'll let you go when you calm down.' At this age, as soon as they show signs of relenting, or mumble a few words of apology, let them out. Make it easy for them to get it right. For example, if they are throwing a toy at the wall and you want them to put it in the box, bring the box close.

3. As children get older (two or three plus), the conversation they have with you gets more important. Remember, they have to convince you that things are going to be different. They have to 'talk their way out' and convince you they can act differently. Another good name for this is 'dealing'. They are learning to 'deal'. Tell them their task – 'Stand there and think about what you did to get into this trouble. As soon as you've figured it out, I'll come and we'll talk about it.'

How to use the 'stand and think' and 'dealing' method

4. The dealing conversation. Ask them:
   a) 'What did you do?' Owning up to one's actions is important.
   b) 'What were you feeling or needing?'
   c) 'What should you have done to meet your needs?' Do they know a better way? Have you discussed this before? Perhaps you will need to teach them. For example, maybe they could join in a game others are playing, use a timer to share a toy fairly, put toys where a baby won't wreck them.
   d) 'What are you going to do in future?' Getting a commitment.
   e) 'Show me.' Go ahead and do it right now – get it right this time.

5. Aim for a happy ending. The beauty of 'dealing' properly like this is that the issue is resolved. You invest some time right now, and the problem need never recur (well, maybe once or twice). You'll know that this was successful because you end up feeling better, and your child feels better. Everyone is redeemed.

A whole new approach

This is a very different form of discipline from those that have been used in the past. When we look back to our childhoods, many of us associate discipline with feeling bad. The history of parenting since the Industrial Revolution has often been one of cruelty and distress for children. Many parents in the old days had little skill, and often simply repeated what was done to them (even though they had hated it at the time).

Once discipline is understood properly there is no need for hurt, shame or fear. The methods of firmlove are part of a breakthrough that is spreading all over the world. Good parents have intuitively found these approaches throughout history, but they have rarely been spelt out in a way that can be learned.

Firmlove methods are respectful of children, are non-violent, and yet clearly place parents in charge. We believe these methods can bring about a revolution in childrearing, making it easier and much more enjoyable to produce young adults who are strong, loving and safe.

Many confrontations can be prevented. If you think ahead, you can often prevent situations from reaching confrontation level. To begin with you may need to use 'stand and think' at least a dozen times a day with little children. Soon, though, they learn to act on an early warning, or a count of '1, 2, 3'. A lot of the time, experienced parents find they can prevent problems by some forethought, and divert them when they do happen, so that confrontations are kept to a manageable minimum. This means that as children get to three or four, you can save your firmlove skills (and your energy) for the times once or twice a day when some important lesson needs to be addressed. Here are some ways to avoid problems – some of the time.

The three tricks of getting cooperation

PREVENTION

A lot of kid trouble arises out of stress, fatigue and hunger.

Make sure you and your child have a good feed before going out, and stop for snacks regularly. Avoid really high-sugar or coloured foods, except as an occasional treat or after eating a meal. Most kids get zippy and harder to manage after a big sugar 'hit'.

Time your activities and leave out non-essentials, so that you are not pressured and having to race the clock. While raising toddlers, it's important to simplify your life. Little things suddenly take a lot longer to do, so do yourself a favour and allow for this.

Make your day ritualized and pleasantly rhythmic, so that kids get used to the routine. When getting ready for school or kindergarten, tell your kids to dress themselves first, before they eat breakfast. This avoids delays and hassles about dressing – hungry kids dress quickly without making a fuss. (To get them to eat a good breakfast is simple – just give them a light tea the night before. They will wake up ravenous!)

Make time at home happy. Have a fun time doing ordinary things – play boppy music while doing the housework. Slow down your expectations of perfection. Be a happy slob. You only have kids full-time for five years, and half-time for about ten years more. Why not enjoy it?

Sometimes little children who are restless just need more exercise – the modern world of small gardens, car seat belts, long drives and a dangerous environment are two-thirds of the problem. Sandpits, water play, room to run and climb make a huge difference. An exhausted child is a cooperative child.

DIVERSION

Often trouble can be avoided by finding a better way, striking a bargain, even bribery – 'I'll buy you some chips at the shop but you'll have to help me and get into your car seat.' A child fighting another over a toy can be offered a longer turn if they go second. Kids can learn to use a timer, to take turns, to play in such a way that both can participate. Sometimes boredom is the real problem, and you can increase the interest by adding a new element – and soon have them cooperating again.

A lot of 'naughtiness' is children just not knowing the right way to do things. Be prepared to teach rather than go on the attack when kids do something that isn't right.

For instance, picture a picnic table at the park. A couple of families are eating together. The eight-year-old boy grabs the last three pieces of chicken from the dish with both hands. Parent number one yells, 'Get out of there you guts!' and takes a swipe at him with a ladle. Good-humoured, but not likely to change his behaviour. Parent number two says, 'Hold on, you haven't checked if anyone else wants some. How about you take one piece and eat that. Then ask later if the rest is free.'

You teach your kids what good behaviour is. How else will they find out?

CONFRONTING

When you have tried all of the above and still your child is being difficult, then it may well mean that your child is asking for a confrontation. So why not give them one? Sometimes children set up conflicts from an inner need to experience safe, strong boundaries. At other times they just aren't able, without the help of our discipline, to handle a problem like sharing, waiting, not hitting, and so on. These are the times to use 'stand and think'. After all, a kid's life is pretty good, and it's not unfair if they have to cooperate sometimes whether they like it or not.

Whether the problem is sharing toys, being gentle, using words and not hitting, being patient, helping out, being obedient in an emergency, learning to join in a game, or whatever, 'stand and think' followed by 'dealing' helps them to stop their first impulse, think it through, and choose a course of action that is going to work. We are aiming not to 'shut down' their behaviour, but to make it more effective.

'So you wanted to join in the game the other kids were playing?' 'Yep.' 'So you threw stones at the other children?' 'Yep.' 'Did you notice that that didn't make them more friendly?' 'Hmm!'

Raising little children is easier if you have a goal to aim for. You are working on producing, by age five or so, a civilized little boy or girl who can go to school, stay at a friend's place, mix well with other kids, and talk to adults in a comfortable way. They'll still have lots to learn, but will be well started.

From toddler to nice person in three short years

In our illustration below, the Stone Age Toddler, accustomed to being the 'centre of the known universe', starts in the left-hand position. That's all right for a little baby, but not good as a life plan. The aim of the discipline game is to have children over at the right-hand

I want it and I want it now. I am King of the Universe! If you don't give it me I'll scream!

I can't always get what I want. I get a lot of good things anyway. Other people have feelings too. If I think before I act, I get better results.

position by the age of five, ready to start school. Always remember that your child really wants to be kind, friendly and cooperative – but needs help to learn how. Expect lots of repetition, but also a sense of steady progress. And always have lots of fun and nice times in between the hassling.

All toddlers are difficult. You don't want to crush them just because they are showing strength. On the other hand, you don't want always to give in to them, because that teaches them that if they fuss and whine they will get their way. So it's a matter of being persistent and good-humoured.

Getting the firmlove attitude The need for firmlove comes on in a big way when your child is around one-and-a-half to two years old. The arrival of 'naughtiness' can be disconcerting for the parent who just wants everything to be happy and gentle. Your baby shifts from an adorable if (demanding) little bundle to a mobile tank on legs.

It's a mental switch you just have to make. For parents of toddlers, firmlove involves realizing that, while you have just spent the last eighteen months trying to make your child happy, you suddenly have quite the opposite situation. You must now, if you are doing your job, make them quite unhappy – dozens of times a day at first, though hopefully only for a few minutes at a time.

> They will usually 'help' you with this by choosing to do something really 'unignorable' such as emptying the fridge or climbing into pot plants.

The attitude you need is tough on the outside, relaxed on the inside. Don't let them think they are cute when they are being defiant or mischievous. It'll take weeks to undo the damage. Drop your voice, look serious, but at the same time feel good that they are gaining lots of learning from having this discipline altercation.

While softlove opens a child's heart, firmlove gives them more backbone so that they will be strong and clear in the world as they grow up.

One day at the supermarket I decided that because my two-year-old daughter was fussing I would let her get off the trolley and walk around the aisles with me. This was a big mistake! She not only ran amok, she also expected the same thing for the next four shopping trips. Toddlers have memories like elephants!

What if I just give in for the sake of peace and quiet?

Sometimes we want to take the easy way out. But this just teaches children to want more, and to whinge and whine harder. Think about it from the two-year-old's point of view. They have been, for the first year, the absolute centre of the universe. What they needed, they got. But now their wants have become more diverse and extreme. They don't just want to be fed, cuddled and changed. They want to dress the dog in your tights. They want to mix all the shampoo and conditioner into a slippery slide on the bathroom floor. They want to play in the traffic. You have to stop them, if only for their own good.

And it *is* for their own good. Because one of the most important lessons of life is being learned at this age – that, while you are loved and wanted, you are only one person among many and you have to get along with others too.

Getting discipline to work smoothly is easy if you understand what to expect and what is going to work at different ages.

How soon does discipline begin?

BABIES

Little Lukah doesn't need discipline. He is four months old. He is not yet able to crawl. He grins and plays with a rattle, and pulls things to himself. He also cries (many times a day) because he is a normal baby and that is how normal babies communicate their needs. His needs are simple – he cries when he is hungry, he cries when he is lonely, he cries when he is wet, he cries if his tummy hurts, and he cries when he is

HAVING LIKEABLE KIDS, ONE GOAL AT A TIME

Jodie, a participant in one of our courses, was very frank. 'I don't like children,' she said. 'I've got three, and what I've found is that I just don't like kids after all!' This is a problem, because if Jodie doesn't like her own children, how will anyone else like them? It's her job to turn them into kids that are likable.

To help her, we get more specific. What changes will each child need to make so that Jodie can like them? We make a list.

1. Her two-year-old will stop hitting and biting.
2. Her four-year-old will stop whingeing and complaining.
3. Her five-year-old will learn to carry out instructions the first time he is asked.

Softlove comes before firmlove, and we realize that Jodie is quite exhausted and will need time out for herself one day a week, as well as extra help from her husband. They resolve to give each other more care and attention, and practise firmlove skills together so they can back each other up. He will reduce his working hours from fifty hours a week to forty-five, so as to do this. Having well-behaved kids will make him happier to spend more time at home.

When we see Jodie six months later, she is looking much more relaxed and peaceful. Her life is still hard work, but she is being gentler on herself, and feeling much more successful with the kids.

bored. That adds up to a lot of crying, but if his mum and dad are on the ball they soon know what is probably needed and are in there at the first whimper to fix him up.

Lukah's dad explains that he was a very high-need baby: 'The big problem was getting him back to sleep – I had to put him on my shoulder and go for a walk around the neighbourhood. Once, at about 4 a.m. the police pulled me up because I looked like a burglar with a swag bag.'

Babies can be hard work, but they are not being naughty – they are just trying to let you know their needs. They don't need discipline, just lots of understanding. And what parents need is sleep.

TODDLERS

Babies' abilities quickly grow until soon they are crawling and then walking about, grabbing and pulling, chomping and poking everything in sight. The whole bottom half of your house is their domain. They are also discovering the use of words to make things happen – 'Bottle!' 'Gimme teddy!' 'Hugga me!'.

With their new skills and mobility, your child is starting to do things and want things which you can't possibly allow. So 'misbehaviour' emerges for the first time. A little baby doesn't deliberately misbehave – but a toddler is a different matter. Your toddler will walk over to the forbidden place or thing, and flash you a grin that says, 'Whatya gonna do about it?' You say, 'No,' and they smile, 'Oh yeah? Stop me.'

Toddlers choose exactly what will 'get your goat', because deep down they are wanting to be stopped. This is an unconscious message saying, 'I need some limits, Mum and Dad. Please stop me going berserk.' (Teenagers too send this message, and we'll talk about them in a little while.)

It isn't all pure rebellion (though some of it is). Sometimes a toddler will just find it too hard to handle the demands of day-to-day life. Sometimes they will just be tired or hungry, and best put down for a sleep or given a snack – their mood will soon improve. Perhaps they will not want to be strapped into their car seat to go to the shops when something good is going on in the yard. Or they will want to crawl across the dinner table to sample what's on their big brother's plate.

A kind parent uses all kinds of tricks to cajole a kiddy along, and a lot of the time this is just what is needed. For instance, one mother saved me a lot of trouble by explaining that if you give your toddler something delicious but time-consuming to eat when you go into the supermarket, they will sit happily in the trolley for twenty minutes. All the same, there will still be times when a child just has to be confronted and do what they are told, because 'I say so'. This age is definitely the firmlove fiesta.

PRESCHOOLERS AND OLDER CHILDREN

As children get beyond the toddler stage, you'll need to use 'stand and think' far less often (thank goodness). Children will 'deal' with you straight away most of the time. Listen to their side of the story – what they were feeling or needing – as it might well be valid. If they can make a good case, then obviously you don't make them do things just because you want to be 'the winner'. They will learn that it's OK to have feelings or needs, but that sometimes they can't get what they want or maybe they can if they go about it in a more acceptable way. Always find out from them what they were feeling (the feelings that led to them playing up), and use firmlove in a kind way so that they know you really want to help, not just persecute them.

TEENAGERS

Despite what people think, adolescents are generally beautiful, cooperative, interesting people. But they are still needing lots of involvement, and this includes some confrontations from time to time. It isn't right to use physical force with teenagers in any way, unless things are severe and you have professional help. So 'stand and think' becomes 'sit and talk'. For example . . .

What time did you come in last night?

Uh, about one?

That's what I noticed. When did you agree you would be in by?

I said twelve, but it was hard to get a lift. The others wanted to stay.

So you couldn't get a lift and that made you late?

Yeah. Can I watch TV now?

Not so fast. How come you made a promise to me that you couldn't keep?

Well, I can't make the others bring me home!

Did you know that could happen when you made the promise?

Uhh, well, I didn't know.

So you made a deal you couldn't really keep.

Uhh, well, I guess so.

So how can we fix that in future? You do want to go out in future?

Huh! Yes I do!

. . . and so on.

In the brain of a teenager around thirteen years of age, everything is suddenly rewired. Puberty is setting in, and it makes them like a newborn baby. They can become forgetful, disorganized and slightly 'out of their tree'. On the plus side, the changes combine to make them very 'soft'. Thirteen-year-olds can be trusting and affectionate – so it can be a chance to get close to them and rebond. Especially if you were hassled and busy when they were babies, this can be a time to build greater closeness.

Enjoy this time, because the 'dopey thirteens' soon give way to the 'cyclone season' of the fourteens. Fourteen-year-olds can be like emotional two-year-olds – testing limits, wanting to struggle with you and needing you to struggle back. The last thing you should do is ignore them. They are wanting independence but needing to learn to be responsible and careful – a peak time for parenting input.

So for fourteen-year-olds firmlove comes into play once again, only this time about different issues – what time to be home at night, picking up your clothes, cooking meals for the family and keeping promises and agreements. The methods of firmlove you use with teenagers are different from the ones you used with toddlers, but the principle is the same. 'I will be firm with you, so you will learn to be a responsible person and know how to handle the real world' is what you are thinking. 'No dishes, no dinner!' is what you are saying.

Teenagers are a big topic, which we can only touch on in this book. It is clear, though, that by getting softlove and firmlove working well with little children and school-age children, you will have a good foundation for handling adolescence when it comes along.

Q. *What about a child who has not been disciplined much before, and is very naughty? I've tried lots of things and nothing works.*
A. If you are introducing 'stand and think' to a child who is very disobedient, then wait till you are ready. Make sure it is a good day when you have someone there to help you and are clear in your mind what you want to achieve.

When and if a problem arises, give the child the chance to fix it. If they don't do that, explain that this will be a new way of dealing with problems. Walk them to the spot you have chosen and say something like, 'You [threw the cake, hit your sister] and you have to stand here and think about it – why you did it, why it's a problem and how you can fix it.' If they try to move away, then hold them firmly, but safely without hurting.

Expect some dramatics. It's a bit of a shock to a child used to running amok. So decide to 'stay with it' even through their loudness and struggling.

Questions parents often ask about 'stand and think' and 'dealing'

Always be firm without hurting. Say to them, 'I will let you go when you stand still', then do it immediately they comply.

Keep it simple and make it winnable. The first time, be happy with a small improvement – a quick 'Sorry' or a token effort is enough the first time.

They will calm down.

They will cooperate.

They will be praised for the new behaviour.

And you will have a little lie down afterwards if you need it!

Next time, it will be a lot easier.

Q. *Should I hold them in the thinking spot if they won't stay there?*
A. If they are little (one-and-a-half to two-and-a-half) allow them to sit or lie down – as long as they stay put. Stay close by and catch them and put them back if they try to 'escape'. You will probably only need to do this once or twice. When they are ready to talk, ask them to stand up and turn around to talk to you. An older child should stand quietly facing the wall, not propped up against it. Physically this keeps the child's attention on the one thing they should be thinking about. They literally aren't squirming around the problem, but are 'standing up' to the task you have given them. Explain that only when he or she does this will you be willing to talk to them.

Q. How old should a child be when you use this method?

A. For you to be using this method, a child needs to have a certain amount of understanding and language. If they can say 'Sorry', 'Not hit' or 'Hands off video' then they've got the message. Tell them they can come out now and get on with doing something pleasant. You can cuddle and calm them afterwards, but don't make a big fuss. The aim is to let it go and get on with life. Until a child has these talking skills, you have to use more baby methods, like diversion!

Q. Why stand up, and why use a corner?

A. This is for simple reasons. It cuts out other distractions and helps the child to focus their attention. It is boring to face the wall, and your legs get tired in a minute or so just standing still. It isn't meant to be either painful or embarrassing. The aim is to get the child motivated to solve the problem and get out of there. Tell them, 'You don't have to feel bad, you're there to think about what you should have done. As soon as you have figured it out, we'll talk and you can come out.'

Away from home, or once your child is really used to standing still when told to, you don't need a wall or corner. You can simply say, 'Stand there and think', in any location.

Q. My child says he's sorry, and then does it all over again.

A. The older they get, the more they try you out – it's the sign of a smart kid. Expect the following confidence tricks:

- I can't stand and think – I have to go to the toilet.
- You don't understand me.
- You don't love me.
- I can't remember.

This child is *not* sorry.

This child is ready to deal.

Don't be fooled. They have to convince you (before you let them out) that they really are feeling sorry, and really are going to change. Through watching their body language, and through being alert during the dealing conversation, you will soon know if they are genuine.

Q. *Can schools use this method?*

A. Yes, but only with some important modifications. 'Stand and think' would be humiliating in front of peers other than brothers and sisters in a family setting. Many primary schools we have consulted with now use a 'thinking place' which is a chair, mat, stool or beanbag. The thinking place isn't especially conspicuous, and shouldn't have a humiliating name like 'naughty chair'. The thinking place is used in the same way – to remove a child from the action, give them time and motivation to think, and keep them close by where you can see from their body language if they are ready to 'deal'.

And always a teacher or principal should deal with them soon. It isn't a sentence they are serving. Kids who play up do need your attention, so give it to them, through dealing with what happened. Remember also to give them attention when they are doing the right thing.

Often in school, a round-table discussion with affected children can be held on a mat or at a table. Problem-solving skills are as important as the three Rs.

What about the old ways of discipline?

There has been a gradual evolution of discipline techniques in the last fifty years.

HITTING AND HURTING

This was the old way. It made children frightened, it eroded any loving relationship, and it taught children that it's OK to hit if you are bigger. Children who were hit became fearful or broken-spirited, or they got angrier and struck back. Sometimes when these children grew up, their own children, wives and others copped the anger that had been stored in their bodies. Violent methods are harmful and have no benefit. In some countries, they are against the law.

SHAMING AND BLAMING

When parents rightly began to reject hitting and smacking in the 1950s, they sometimes had no other tools to put in their place, and few skills in communication. So they often used shame, fear, blame – calling their children no good, and a million other names. The result was a damaged self, a wounding of the spirit. Shaming and blaming were often a failure as discipline too, because children became what they were called – lazy, stupid, selfish, fat, whatever. Kids who were shamed went one of two ways – either depressed and guilty, or rebellious and angry.

REWARDS AND CONSEQUENCES

A good example of these are star charts, where a child gets stars for good behaviour, usually building up to some reward at the end of the week or when they have enough stars. Star charts can work well because they help parents focus on the positive, and they help the child have smaller goals to aim for. With some children this can make a lot of difference.

Pocket money in a small quantity, some jobs which you just 'have to' do as your part in the family, and extra pay for doing extra jobs, is a mix of rewards which many families have found works well because it resembles the real world.

Similarly, 'natural consequences' work by letting the child have the problem they create – changing the sheets if they wet the bed, getting into trouble if they are late for school, and so on. As children get older, they are more and more able to learn from the results of their actions and it is important that parents allow this to happen. Natural consequences aren't enough on their own – for example, the consequence of running on the road would not be a good idea.

TIME OUT

Time out has become a popular recommendation of parenting experts. It means sending your child to their room, usually for about five minutes, to cool off. It has literally saved a lot of children's lives, because it gives parents time to cool off too. So it is a coping strategy, and useful to almost everyone at times. I use it myself with a toddler when I am hot and bothered and just want some peace for a few minutes. But in itself time out is not a discipline method because it doesn't involve teaching or thinking about change.

Here are some examples of what parents tell us about time out: 'It doesn't work because my child has fun in their room, they have so many toys!' or 'He smashes the room up, breaks things, and sometimes gets out of the window' or 'It works well for me – mainly as a chance to cool off. But it doesn't always change the behaviour. She often just does it all again ten minutes later.'

The key differences between 'time out' and 'stand and think' are:

1. 'Stand and think' is quicker. When the child is in the corner in the same room with you, you are able to see straight away when they have finished thinking about their behaviour. It encourages rapid resolution.
2. There are no distractions with 'stand and think'. The child stays put until they do the thinking they need to do. It keeps the problem with the child.
3. 'Stand and think' isn't a punishment. It's a thinking and teaching time. It doesn't create resentment. The child can end the process by cooperating at any time, and so is usually out within a minute or two.
4. 'Dealing' creates closeness, not distance. Naughty kids don't need isolation – they usually need more intense contact. The dealing conversation shows that you care, and you want to help them solve their problems.

We recommend that you only use time out if you feel you are in danger of hitting your child, or otherwise really need a break. In fact, you can use it preventively by saying, 'I want us both to cool down now. Please go to your room and play quietly.' You may wish to have a 'dealing' conversation afterwards, so that you know something has been changed.

Some childhood dilemmas aren't so much discipline questions as values questions. You want your child to decide for themselves what is the right thing to do. You can't make kids take on your values. But you can help them figure out all the angles about their behaviour. In the long run, this means they will do the right thing when you are not around, because they believe it is the right thing.

Helping older children with moral decisions

Sara, aged nine, was asked by a friend to go to her sleepover. She happily agreed. Her friend, a shy girl, was really pleased that Sara had accepted – there were only three girls attending.

Then, out of the blue, Sara was invited to a church camping weekend by another friend – but it clashed with the date of the sleepover. Sara really wanted to go on the camp, but it meant breaking her acceptance of the sleepover. Her parents didn't force her to keep the agreement – that would have just led to sulking. But they discussed the two parts of the problem with her:

1. Respecting her friend's feelings.
2. Keeping an agreement.

These were important principles. Sara's parents gently pointed out that 'something better has come up' is no excuse for disappointing someone who is counting on you. They also said it was Sara's decision, and they wouldn't hassle her once she had decided. Sara reluctantly declined the camping trip, and had fun at the sleepover. Her parents felt really proud of her for showing so much character.

Children and teenagers won't always make the decision you are hoping for. But making mistakes is part of the lesson. Also, it's just remotely possible that you might be wrong and that they might be right – a sobering thought!

Should I smack? – an important decision every parent has to make

It's getting dark, and the road is heavy with traffic going home for the night. People hurry along the footpath and a light rain has begun to fall. A little child's yelling catches my attention – a young mother is talking at a public phone outside a shop, at the same time trying to keep her toddler in check. He wants to run and play at the kerb, where rainwater is gurgling and splashing. But the cars and trucks are dangerously close by. You can feel her frustration – she is alternately raging angrily with whoever is on the phone, then shouting at her youngster that she will 'teach him to behave'. He whinges and struggles to pull free. Then it's all too much. She drops the phone, grabs the neck of his tiny jacket, and gives him a backhanded blow across the face that makes his head spin.

ATTITUDES HAVE CHANGED

It used to be an everyday event, forty or fifty years ago, to see children being beaten by adults. People did it in public, and nobody much batted an eyelid. Attitudes to hitting children have changed, just as they have changed to men hitting women. Today, a bruised child is a police matter. Eighty per cent of parents say they still smack their children occasionally, but most would prefer not to.

There are still many people, though, who advocate a smack as a way to get quick results. Perhaps it's time for us to make a personal choice about what happens to our kids – especially now that better forms of discipline are available to us. We believe that if parents knew of a better form of discipline, they would never smack again.

Are beating and smacking the same? Isn't smacking just a little bit of needed discipline? Often when I give a talk about discipline, someone will come up to me and say, 'I got plenty of hidings when I was a kid, and they never hurt me!' My guess – based partly on the very passion with which these people speak – is that it did hurt them, and it still is hurting. Pretending it didn't hurt is the child's first defence against humiliation. And the anger they hold inside comes out later in many different ways.

It's time we were more honest about this whole issue. From a child's viewpoint, smacking is scary and humiliating. From a parent's point of view, it is risky. Risky because there isn't any clear-cut point where a smack becomes a hit, and a hit becomes an angry venting of parental frustration. How do we know how much is enough? Can we honestly say when we are hitting for the child's 'benefit', and when it's just to make us feel better? Or to get revenge? Can we honestly say it's just the child we're angry with, and not a lot of things rolled into one?

The bottom line(!) is that smacking really doesn't work, except in the very short term. It eats away at love and trust – so children get crankier still. I have seen lots of children – who defiantly say, 'It didn't hurt! I don't care!' – learn to become immune to it. The parents who lay into their children in the street or supermarket are clearly losing control of their children, not gaining it.

WHY DO PARENTS SMACK THEIR KIDS?

The fact of it is, if we're honest, we hit children because of our own needs. We are scared of losing control over them. Or, often with young children, our nurturing energy just runs out. We feel exhausted, sleep-deprived, we never have a moment to ourselves. The slap is just our inner self striking back, saying 'I've got needs too.' It can be a self-protection instinct – they've just jabbed you in the eye as you put them in their car seat, or banged you with a spoon as you straighten their bib.

At this age, children can't always understand or notice our feelings or our words to them. Yet we feel a strong urge to make an impact, to have an effect on their behaviour. So smacking or hitting them to 'get their attention' is a natural urge. We need to resist this urge, and can do so if we improve our skills in connecting with children and making them take notice.

Some smacking advocates are compassionate and concerned people. They often argue that, if not controlled early by a light tap, children will become even naughtier, until their parent loses all patience and gives them a real hiding. Their theory is that little hits prevent big ones. However, our experience is that parents who give little hidings also give big ones – the little hidings soon don't work. Kids get resentful, they hit their own brothers and sisters, or hit you back. It's important to draw the line, and the realistic place to draw it is back at square one. If we decide *never* to hit our children – as I and many people I know have done – then we are committed to finding better ways.

DISCIPLINE WITHOUT SMACKING

We do have to discipline children. And words alone are not enough with very little ones. It's certainly necessary sometimes to hold and restrain little children to help them to calm down and behave. This can be done quite safely. 'Stand and think' has been adopted successfully by thousands of parents. It's a matter of training your child as they grow up. And there will still be 'impossible' times in the rain in the street, where it's just a matter of 'pick up and carry'. You have to keep your sense of humour. It's lucky toddlers are small – it makes them portable.

By the time adolescence comes along, there should never be any need for fear or intimidation. If kids run away from home, or are violently defiant, this almost always means that communication has broken down years back, and parents have been relying on aggression rather than a mixture of love and assertiveness.

Many people block out the memory of the pain they felt as children – and so go on inflicting this pain on their kids. As a counsellor, I know what pain is involved. I have heard too many people talk – with tears in their eyes – about the humiliation and fear they felt when a parent went out of control. My patients show me the broken blood vessels in their legs from being 'smacked' as children. Hairdressers tell me many of their clients have nicks and bare spots and scars under their hairline from blows on the head when they were little. The scars are even bigger on the inside – if a child cannot feel safe and secure with its own parents, how can it feel safe in the world?

There's another reason to stop hitting children. Evidence is mounting that children who feel safe with their parents will tell their parents if something is wrong – for instance, if they have been sexually assaulted. When parents routinely use fear and shame as discipline tools, then children will feel unsafe to tell, in case they get the blame. Kids who are never frightened or harmed by their parents will always see their parents primarily as protectors. They will feel safer to say, 'No – I'll tell!' to somebody else, and avoid abuse in the first place.

MAKING THE DECISION

We think that it is time for us as parents to abandon hitting as a way of controlling children.

The first step is simple. You make a personal commitment never to hit a child again. The automatic effect is that you become committed to finding non-violent discipline methods that work. Such methods exist, and are able to be mastered.

While raising our first child, we found ourselves giving little smacks for certain behaviour – things like touching the heater. Being a strong-willed child, our son was not impressed by this and made a habit of repeating the behaviour. We found that we were miserable about making him cry, and we weren't teaching him much either. So we began to search for alternatives. We discovered that some parents *never* smacked their children, and that in fact there were whole countries where it was illegal to smack a child. We also learned the firm and clear forms of discipline taught in this book, and used by thousands of parents around the world, and began putting them into practice at our place. We are eternally grateful to have found a better way.

We are all yearning for a peaceful world – where conflicts can be negotiated non-violently. We need to start at the beginning. If we can't manage it at home, we will never manage it in the Middle East.

If you find yourself in agreement, you can make this commitment too. Your child will come to know that their mother or father will never, ever, physically harm them. That they are safe in their own home. What a beautiful way to be.

Conclusion By using firmlove methods, you can win both ways. You can give up on smacking and blaming, which no one really enjoys. And yet you can have a household where the adults are in charge, and the kids do what they are told when necessary. Your kids will still be normal – two-year-olds will still be hard work, and fourteen-year-olds will still be cyclonic. But by knowing how to respond you can address these stages confidently and clearly, and then get on with the enjoyable and pleasant parts of family life.

Remember – always and only do what works best for you. 'Stand and think' and 'dealing' are just two more possible strings to your bow. As this letter from a family indicates, they can make a lot of difference:

> Dear Steve and Shaaron,
>
> We attended your seminar in October, and thoroughly enjoyed the session. I still keep in touch with another lady I met there.
>
> Your seminar came at an appropriate time because we didn't want to beat our son Carey, but didn't know what to do. Now Carey (twenty-eight months) stands himself in 'the corner' and says 'I'm thinking about it' and the tears in our eyes are from joy – he's so cute!
>
> Marion and David

4

Who will raise your children?

Taking care with childcare

It's 9.30 in the morning when the phone rings. On the line is a young professional woman whom I know only slightly. She is in tears. She has just left her four-month-old baby boy at a child-care centre for the first time, and is now sitting at her desk on her first day back at work.

The baby was distressed to be left, she was anguished to leave him. She can't concentrate on her work – all she can think of is her baby, who has scarcely been away from her in his whole short life. What should she do?

Doing what your heart says Many people would say to the young mother returning to work, 'What's the problem? The child will soon settle down.' After all, this can happen with a five-year-old, too, on their first day at school, and they are usually soon over it and settling in happily. Shouldn't she just put it out of her mind and concentrate on her job and her workmates?

As we talk it over, it emerges that it isn't just a problem of a tearful parting. This young woman has a deep ambivalence about returning to work.

We discuss the pressures on her, trying to separate what are her own feelings and what are the wishes of others around her. Many of her friends have their babies cared for in creches and are working. Her husband wants her to go back to work – the money will be welcome. Her employer wants her back at work – she has only been away five months in total.

But as she talks it's clear that she is not happy. What she wants is to be with her child. Gradually, she begins to settle on what she will do. She decides to meet with her boss and explain that she has changed her plans, to apologize for this, and thank him for being understanding. After negotiation with her boss, she in fact takes a whole further year off, and then returns only part-time. She's lucky – to be a skilled person, and to have a partner whose income can support the family – so that she can choose to do this. She is enormously relieved to be following her own heart, and not the 'shoulds' put on to her by society and those around her.

From time immemorial, most children have been raised close to home by a combination of their parents and close relatives, in a village or neighbourhood setting. So the work (and the pleasure) of raising children was shared amongst those who loved them. Throughout the non-industrial world, even today, children and adults spend their days together. You will see mothers at work with babies in slings, and little children accompanying men to work in the fields. It is only in the Western world that we shut our children (and our old people) away from the mainstream of life.

Childcare – a new invention

One hundred years ago most men worked with their wives and families close by – the vast majority of British men worked within walking distance of home. Then, with industrialization men began to travel to distant work leaving women and children, often isolated and lonely, at home. In the 1960s women decided they wanted to work too, and joined men in a flight from the home.

Reduced wages, single parenthood and unemployment have meant that many women *have* to work, as well as raise a family. To deal with this, there has been a rapid upsurge in childcare provisions of various kinds. Today, we talk of the childcare 'industry' and finding suitable childcare is a subject close to the heart of almost every parent.

So today's parents have an option that in the past was only available to the extremely wealthy. We can pay professionals to mind our children all day. If you can overcome the problems of waiting lists, the cross-city drives and your fears about quality of care, then, encouraged by strong ideologies about your rights to do so, you may have your children cared for from birth to adulthood by complete strangers at a cost. (Once at school they can have before- and after-school care, holiday care, and Saturday schools. You hardly need to see them!)

The second biggest decision a parent makes The decision to have children is probably the biggest decision you ever make in your life. Deciding who will *raise* your children is the second biggest. We use the word 'raise' because the first five years are well-known to be the time of maximum intellectual and emotional growth. Children who go into care at two or three months of age, and stay for seven or eight hours a day, are basically spending their childhood in care. What kind of person they become – how they are comforted, how they are disciplined, what values and attitudes they will take on – will be the composite of the input of a large number of people, with widely varying styles and values. These children will certainly be adaptable! But will they be capable of intimacy? How will they integrate all these messages?

70

The two big questions – whether to have children, and who will care for them – are interlinked. As more than one crèche director has told us in private (after fighting off the pressure from parents to take younger and younger babies for longer and longer hours), 'I don't know why some of these people have children at all!' It's a fair comment.

In the last ten years a kind of 'cuckoo culture' has developed. (Cuckoos are birds which lay their eggs in other birds' nests to be raised by them.) This trend has been encouraged through young women's magazines, and by media role models who portray this lifestyle as ideal. In some circles, having your kids raised for you is seen as a measure of success – the desirable norm.

The cuckoo culture

We are a society that worships 'freedom', including freedom from the inconvenience of children. At the extreme end of the spectrum, there are sections of British society where children have become little more than a fashion accessory – window-dressing – wheeled out for a photo opportunity and then shuffled off to be attended to by others. It's fashionable to 'have' kids, but not necessarily to be encumbered by them.

We humans are very conformist creatures, and the perception that 'everyone does it' makes childcare as a choice seem harmless or even beneficial. So fashion, as much as real hard data, often influences these important decisions.

While the growth of this 'arm's length' parenting is a worry, the vast majority of parents are not like this. Most parents do want to raise their own children, do want the best for them, and are willing to sacrifice career aspirations and recreational or social goals to a high degree to achieve these aims. Increasingly men – even those in public life – are making decisions that favour parenthood over career.

Sadly, many parents feel forced by economic need to return to work when their children are young. They do so with immense regret. Others are confused, wanting to provide a nice home, toys, school fees, but not wanting to miss out on time with their children either. Whatever the reason, we need to know the real cost before making a decision.

I had originally planned to write this chapter as an objective look at the childcare choices parents can make. It was the safe way – to sum up the

A personal view

arguments in what has been a long and worrying debate, and leave you to reach your own conclusions.

I soon realized, though, that to write in this way would have been wrong. I don't make my decisions as a parent by reading statistics or studies. I listen to these, but when it comes to the crunch I go on how I feel. Trusting intuition is what good parenting is all about. I'm guessing that you as a reader would prefer to hear my honest opinion, as opposed to pseudo-scientific fence-sitting.

I have strong concerns about childcare as it is used by many parents today, and believe that the damage it sometimes does to young children is of a hidden and long-term kind.

I am not alone. Professor Jay Belsky, probably the foremost academic in the field, argues that the evidence of damage is subtle; but it is enough that in 1986 he reversed his long-standing support for childcare for children under three. In early 1994, the world's foremost parenting author, Dr Penelope Leach, created a storm of concern by saying similar things, in her book *Children First*. I have always felt uneasy about the presence of babies and toddlers in creches. The more I have talked to people – parents, childcarers and adults who remember their own childhood experiences – the more my inner convictions have been strengthened.

I must stress that I cannot prove what I am about to say. The research hasn't been done yet, but like all parents I can't press a pause button on my children's lives until it's finished. All I can tell you is my point of view, so you can choose to agree, disagree or keep an open mind.

It is my belief that:
1. Long day care of children under three, in an institutional setting like a crèche, will result in those children having a seriously deprived childhood experience. The younger the children are when they enter childcare, and the longer the hours they spend there each day, the more serious will be their deprivation.
2. The problems and deficits will occur in many areas, but especially in those relating to emotional stability

intimacy and trust, and learning to develop lifelong relaxation and a peaceful inner world. This damage will be masked by an apparent gain in superficial social skills which actually reflect the child's strategies for coping with this stressful environment.

3. In the long-term, these deficits will lead especially to problems in forming and keeping long-term relationships. The general mental and physical health of these children is likely to be affected, and when they grow up they may have difficulty bonding with and caring for their own children.

In short, my belief is that, except in those cases of parents who are seriously impaired or genuinely incapable of raising their own children, young children are always better off being cared for by someone who loves them. Professionalism of staff and richness of surroundings, while important, don't touch on the question of love. Young children's bodies can be kept safe and their minds occupied, but their deeper, more subtle needs cannot be met except by someone with a fierce, long-term commitment to them. This is not something you can buy.

The dangers of childcare suggested above have to be set alongside its benefits. It's clear to anyone associated with families:

The plusses of childcare

- That all parents need breaks from the lonely and unnatural world of being at home alone with little children.

- That women have as much right as men to have and develop careers, and to be economically independent.

- That children in day care learn social and other skills, have enriched input and stimulation, and in many cases love and enjoy their time in crèches, family day care, or other childcare situations.

- That some parents are so ill equipped (materially or personally) that children are safer, happier and better off being cared for professionally for most of the time.

These plusses are well documented, and widely accepted.

Fearlessly facing the facts

The plusses are real, but so are the negatives. For a long time, however, the negatives have been suppressed – for fear of making parents feel guilty, or for fear of inviting even closer scrutiny and questioning of the childcare 'industry'. I think the first reason is patronizing, and the second is dishonest.

Childcare professionals often have a well-intentioned, but (I think) misplaced tendency to protect parents from concern. For example, there has been a long and important campaign by childcare academics and government centres in Australia to bring in national standards of childcare. This campaign was vigorously opposed by the private sector of the industry. A spokeswoman supporting better standards was quoted as saying, 'We didn't want to create hysteria by emphasizing cases where untrained fifteen-year-olds were left in charge of forty-five children.' The intention is admirable, but why should parents be seen as more hysterical than any other group? Parents care intensely about their children, and should be informed.

Is the rapid and widespread adoption of childcare a terrible thing? Or is it a wonderful breakthrough for parents – setting them free to have a better life? Is it a boon for children, given that many of us no longer live close to grandparents and relatives, who used to take this role, to have professionals to care for them (instead of amateurs like their mum and dad)? Or does it represent a serious loss of intimacy and specialness in childhood? Taking a middle road – can childcare be used in a balanced way to augment and enhance early childhood? However we view it, the childcare boom is a huge uncontrolled social experiment, and needs to be looked at with very clear eyes.

In this chapter we'll look at the reasons why people go back to work when their children are little, and whether these reasons are realistic. We'll discuss whether it actually makes more sense – and brings more joy – to stay home for a few years until your children are older.

74

Then we'll look at the realities of what care is available, so that when you do need it you can choose wisely. We'll examine what the hazards of childcare are so that you can analyse whether your child is suffering ill effects. We believe that once you are armed with this information you will be better able to make a choice that is right for you.

'But what if I have no choice?' – mothers who are forced to work

Many mothers with low-income-earning (or unemployed) partners, or single mothers, simply have no choice but to work, even though they would strongly prefer to be with their children. (This is a tragedy of national scale.)

My belief is that children can adapt to difficult circumstances if they understand the necessity. They can also intuit the truth. If your children know you would rather be with them, but that you have no choice, then the effect on their self-esteem is not nearly as severe as if they feel you just aren't interested in them – that you would rather be somewhere else.

Undermining the confidence of young parents

Sometimes young parents returning to work will argue that they are not 'good' at parenting – that their child would be better off with a carer. Yet it isn't as simple as being a good or bad parent – very few of us are good at it to begin with. Through the hours spent together, you become a good parent for that child. That's what a relationship (as opposed to a service) is all about.

Childcare can actually undermine your confidence. Sometimes parents feel that it makes the situation worse. They lose confidence and can be made to feel alienated from their child, not as loving nor as capable or interesting as the childcarer. The better others seem able to handle your baby or toddler, the lower your self-esteem sinks. It is more helpful to work with a parent – to give them skills, teach them more positive interactions and to care for them – rather than to bypass them and care for the baby. It's a sensitive question.

Stability and consistency, the underpinnings of a young child's world, seem impossible to attain in childcare. Even 'quality' care still means your child gets looked after by dozens of different individuals in the course of the four or so years before starting school. In reality, we cannot even organize the same location – a recent study found that some families had to access up to four different kinds of care in an average week to cover the hours they needed. Another study found great inconsistencies between centres, which children had to deal with in the round of a normal day.

Finding a balance that isn't a compromise Life with toddlers in a lonely suburban house or flat can be a recipe for insanity if it is unrelieved by adult contact and activities other than housekeeping and parenting. So, for the wellbeing of adults and children, we need ways of providing safe care.

Friends, family day carers and childcare centres can all work well at different times of a child's life in different combinations to improve a family's life greatly. The key is to know what children's real needs are. This has been the missing piece in the discussion so far. Childcare was invented for the convenience of adults, not the needs or wishes of children. Those were an afterthought.

Research evidence, along with a revival of plain common sense, is leading to a reversal of the idea that a crèche childhood is a good childhood. I predict that there will be a definite move towards the use of childcare to augment parenting (rather than, as it is sometimes used today, as a virtual replacement for it). I also predict (and hope) that the use of childcare for babies and toddlers will be drastically reduced as parents realize the psychological and other costs.

We have left the 'you-can-have-it-all' 1980s, and are now in the 'get-real' 1990s. We are taking a fresh look at many things, and 'arm's length' childraising is one of them. People queueing for a childcare place may soon be met by a rush of people heading the other way.

News release

'Working mothers who send their young children to childcare centres may suffer from high levels of depression because of the separation, a new study has found. Some mothers lapsed into a depression serious enough to justify treatment by a psychiatrist, the study revealed.

'About eighty Melbourne mothers, who were putting their infants aged under two in suburban day care centres while working for financial needs, were interviewed by a University of Melbourne researcher. The study found that within the first two months of using childcare, many women complained of anxiety after being separated from their children. The anxiety sometimes led to depression. Four of the eighty women were suffering from severe clinical depression.

'About one in three of the working mums said they would have preferred to have stayed at home with their child instead of working and leaving their child in day care.'

('Working mums feel the pain of leaving children', *Mercury*, Hobart, 13 February 1993)

SEVEN SHAMELESS REASONS FOR STAYING HOME WHEN YOUR KIDS ARE SMALL!

1. **I'm selfish** – why should someone else enjoy my beautiful children while I slave away to pay for it? Why should they enjoy seeing them take their first steps, and come out with new words? Why should someone else get that glorious affection my children give out? I want it for me!

2. **I'm the best** – no one can raise my kids as well as I can. No one feels about them the way I do. No one knows them like I do.

3. **I'm supercautious** – I'm fastidious about safety, about guarding against abuse, about sensitivity to their feelings and what media they are exposed to. By being around all the time, I don't have to take chances on these issues – I know they are safe.

4. **I enjoy working in a team** – my partner and I work together well, we complement each other in parenting, and I like doing this with him or her. It's something else that makes us closer.

5. **I'm poor and proud** – I have so much self-esteem that I don't need great furniture or expensive clothes or a fancy house and car. I'm such a snob that I don't need money beyond the bare essentials. My kids are my jewellery.

6. **I'm lazy** – by raising secure and unhassled kids who feel safe and settled, I am making it easy for myself later on. I'm planning to cruise through their adolescence. And I'm teaching them fifty kinds of housework.

7. **I'm into it** – I enjoy the progress, the affection, the freedom to set my own pace, to decide how I will spend my time, the social get-togethers with other parents, the effect of the seasons on our activities, how my kids keep me young, and that I am (for this short time) the centre of their world.

There are four main reasons why parents return to work.

1. **Real financial need**

   Many families need both parents to be employed to survive. Many single mothers, too, need to work to provide adequately for their kids. For these families, childcare is a necessity of life. In one survey, 62 per cent of employed mothers indicated they would prefer to stay at home while children are below school age.

2. **Perceived financial need**

   Many couples feel that they need to work, but on closer examination this is based on a desire for a relatively high standard of living. As couples marry later and have children later, perhaps they have grown used to a high disposable income. A few decades ago, 'going without' was a normal part of life with young children and less of a concern. Our media images and expectations, and a competitive (rather than supportive) kind of society, mean that standards of income are much higher than actually required.

3. **Peer pressure**

   Many mothers feel they 'should' go to work, that this is the 'done thing', and that they are somehow defective if they 'just' want to raise children. Feminism has been ambiguous about motherhood, and the nurture of children has sometimes been devalued. For a man to prefer parenting to the full-time paid workforce is also seen as rather unusual.

4. **Enjoyment of career**

   Some mothers find their career so satisfying and enjoyable that it competes favourably with being at home with children. Sometimes their partner is more interested in full-time parenting, and so they reverse roles. At other times, neither partner is so keen on being with the children, and they place their children lower in their priorities.

Clearly, a multi-pronged approach is needed. We still need better-quality childcare, especially for the three to five age group where it is developmentally appropriate. We need the workplace to be much more family friendly, giving men and women parental leave, flexible hours, on-site childcare and 'sick child' leave. This will allow parents to make choices according to their own wisdom about what their family needs, and not be caught in impossible compromises.

If you do have a choice but just don't like parenting

The availability of childcare from babyhood has meant that many people decide to have children, while planning to have the bulk of their care done by others. Other parents feel that they are not really very good at parenting, and so it is better done by others.

But the fact is, many of us are not good parents to begin with. It comes with practice. Parenthood isn't a hobby, and it isn't a fair-weather kind of thing. There may be whole stages of the life cycle that you find very difficult – not all mothers like babies, some people find toddlers impossible, others dislike teenagers, and so on. Every parent at some time feels like giving up and retreating.

But there are usually reasons behind this that are worth getting to the bottom of.

It's in facing up to many crises and not giving in that we learn and really come to know ourselves and find how to be with children in a satisfying and happy way.

In the 1960s, there was some concern about whether institutional childcare harmed children. However, the research seemed reassuring – on the measures used, there was little if any difference. If anything, children in day care were more socially skilled, and somewhat more independent and assertive. Critics of these studies pointed out that almost all studies were of high quality centres, usually on university campuses convenient to the researchers, and far from representative of the real world.

Is there a childcare syndrome? (How can I tell if childcare is harming my child?)

So in the 1970s, the direction swung to investigating what was meant by 'quality', and whether this made a difference. It was found, not surprisingly, that smaller groups, better-educated carers, high staff ratios, all improved the outcomes. There was a risk identified of 'apathy and distress' among infants in larger groups, and 'boredom and tuning out' amongst older children if programmes were not well designed.

In the 1980s, researchers began to suspect that the kind of quality care parents want for their children might just not be possible in a formal setting. A secure, warm attachment to carers emerges again and again as the problem area. Gay Ochiltree, in summing up the research for her book, *Children in Australian Families* (Australian Institute of Family Studies 1992), points out the reality of high staff turnover in centres: 'The loss of an attachment figure can be very painful to a young child. When these observations are juxtaposed with the 40 per cent annual turnover among centre-based childcare providers and 60 per

81

cent turnover among home based providers, there is tremendous cause for concern.'

In a penetrating and careful article, 'Infant Day Care, a Cause for Concern', Jay Belsky (who we mentioned earlier) analysed the entire body of research, collected from hundreds of studies from around the world in all imaginable conditions.

He found that there were suggestions of specific and recurrent damaging effects which emerged in many studies which, if not proven, were strongly indicated, especially when the research picture was looked at as a whole. In particular, he found four outcomes that were of concern in children who had entered childcare *before the age of one*:

- A pattern of withdrawal from and avoidance of the mother figure – babies and toddlers who did not approach their mothers, or see their mothers as sources of reassurance. The childcare experience seemed to make these little ones angry at their mothers, so that they did not turn to her for comfort. Their attachment was either displaced elsewhere, or they did not form strong attachments.

- Heightened aggressiveness – a tendency in the present, as well as later in school life, to use aggression, hitting, swearing, fighting, rather than talking through, walking away, staying calm.

- Non-compliance – ignoring or defying adults' requests or commands, doing the opposite, being rebellious.

- Social withdrawal – walking away, avoiding adult company, keeping to themselves.

These four effects were found across a wide range of studies – impoverished, middle class, upper class, in unstable family day care, high-quality centres, poor-quality centres, and even with at home babysitter care.

The effects are not surprising. Placed in the average childcare centre where other children compete for attention, where adult figures come and go, where the day is noisy and there is no private space, children learn to fend for themselves. They may learn not to place too much trust in adult figures, including their own mother, who is not there for them for much of the day. They cope as best they can, some probably better than others.

For parents, then, the question 'Is childcare harming my child?' can be answered with some clarity. If the child is regularly displaying a combination of the four symptoms listed above, then the answer is probably – 'Yes'.

'YOU CAN SPOT THE CHILDCARE KIDS'

While researching and interviewing parents for this section, we came across some revealing comments from parents who were also primary and infant school teachers.

'You can tell which kids have been in day care and crèches before starting school. They are really different.'

'It's hard to describe – they are kind of colder, less interested in you as a person. They can be quite good at manipulation.'

'Most little ones come along holding Mummy's hand – they are anxious, but they soon pass on the trust from their mother to you (the teacher). They are very affectionate and contactable. Childcare children seem kind of hardened – it's just another person, just another place. You often don't meet their parents either. They might have come from day care, and go back to it after school.'

'You get the impression these children have met lots of adults, and have no special feeling about it any more. They get on all right, get on with the day, but it's with a kind of resigned feeling. They are tougher, almost depressed.'

There are many kinds of childcare options to choose from. Each has pluses and minuses. Let's look at each in turn so you can evaluate which, if any, are suited to your needs.

Comparing the options

WHAT IS A DAYCARE CENTRE LIKE?

Most centres are purpose-built buildings about the size of a large house. They usually open from 8.00 a.m. to 6.00 p.m. or longer if they cater for parents who work shift work. They may offer full-time, part-time and occasional care. Regulations govern staff numbers, children's numbers, space indoors and out, toilets and so on.

Staff ratios are about one adult to five under two-year-olds, and one to fifteen over-twos. Some of the staff, but not all, need to have childcare or early childhood qualifications. Good centres will provide structured programmes similar to preschool activities so that children can learn through guided activity and play.

Fees vary from centre to centre but average about £95 per week. In some circumstances this is largely paid by government subsidy, in others it falls completely on the parents.

Childcare can be both expensive and cheap, depending on your point of view and your circumstances. The government estimates the average annual cost of full-time childcare is £5,200 per child, which is almost a fifth of the after-tax income of the average couple's (dual-income) full-time earnings. For some parents the cost (especially if you include petrol and, in many cases, the need for a second car) and the time involved, actually outweighs what they might earn.

A positive development is crèches provided by employers at the workplace. For giving child and parent easy access – at coffee breaks and lunchtime, for feeds, and in reducing travel time – this is a big improvement. Employers benefit too, from relaxed and happier staff.

REGISTERED CHILDMINDERS

This is a scheme by which local authorities license mothers in their own homes to care for up to five children from other families. Usually only one of these can be a baby; the others will be varied in age. Houses are inspected thoroughly for safety standards – child-safe cupboards, gates, fences and so on. Childminders' supervisors are watchful that good care is being provided, and will not license a childminder who is considered unsatisfactory.

When choosing a minder, the best bet is to look for someone who has been doing it for some time, and seems happy and well-organized. Trust your own feelings around that person, and about that household, and look carefully at the demeanour of the children there.

The huge plus is that childminders offer a home environment, and with luck can become a stable relationship where your child feels they are cared for as an individual. As with any trust relationship, time and getting to know a person are your only guides. If you are lucky, this person may become a family friend as well as a loving addition to your child's life.

Using a registered childminder is more personal than a childcare centre for you too. You can take the time to get to know your child's carer over a cuppa, and become friends as much as possible. It's fine to make a few enquiries and visit a few childminders to see how you 'click'. This is too important a relationship to leave to chance.

Because of the very low rates of pay to childminders for the responsible and skilled work they actually do, it is relatively cheap child care for parents. You can have a child with a childminder for a fifty-hour week for about £80–90 per week. Clearly registered childminders should be subsidized by government to make this an affordable alternative, and a worthwhile career path for carers.

There is a small but important risk in any childcare situation of sexual abuse, perhaps by a husband or older boy or girl in a household, or by workers or visitors at a centre. (Hospital studies have found that 10 per cent of serious abuse takes place in a childcare setting.) One criterion for letting your child be cared for by others is that the child has reached an age where they can tell you clearly if something is wrong.

NURSERY SCHOOLS

Nursery schools are exactly what the name suggests – a part-time introduction to school life for children aged around three to five. Many parents find them a great idea and decide when their child should begin depending on the individual child's readiness.

Nursery schools are a good childcare option for many parents. Since they are an outgrowth of school rather than of the need to have children minded, they are more educationally based than most other centres. Nursery schools usually run only a half-day or short-day session, and most children attend less than five days a week. (It's noteworthy that educationists consider this enough time for young children to be in a structured setting.)

Because of the short hours, nursery schools are ideal for at home parents, but are usually not convenient for employed parents who need longer hours.

NANNIES

Nannies are at-home one-to-one carers chosen and employed by you. This is obviously expensive, and quality is hugely variable. (Do they mind your child, or your TV set?) Nannying is a lonely job for someone who isn't really cut out for it. A caller to the Australian Broadcasting Corporation's *Offspring* programme told of her one-year-old son having three nannies in six months. 'Still,' she said, 'it's not much fun for seventeen-year-old girls being with a baby all day.' (Nor, we might add, is this situation much fun for the baby.) On the plus side, some nannies are superb, and an enormous help to the family unit. And the child is cared for in your home.

There is a side effect to nannies which most parents will be aware of, since it applies to any good-quality care. Studies of nanny use in affluent north American families found that a good nanny actually damaged the child's relationship with its mother, since the child naturally gravitated to the person who provided the warmth and time. It's an understandable problem, but it is really a problem of overuse which could be avoided by balancing time with mother, father and nanny. There is nothing wrong with loving lots of people.

FAMILY AND FRIENDS

By far the largest form of childcare used in Britain is still that provided by family and friends – grandparents, neighbours and so on. This is especially favoured by families of non-British origin, where family and cultural ties tend to be particularly strong and supportive.

When family and friends are caring for children, the same cautions still need to be observed and care must be taken that arrangements are fair to all concerned. But, by and large, children are loved and cared for because they are family, and this timeless way of sharing the joy and work of childrearing has a lot going for it.

DISCIPLINE – A PROBLEM AREA FOR CARERS

The pressure on a carer is to avoid trouble – to sidestep the discipline wrangles that parents at home with kids have to have, and from which children learn important lessons. Children who misbehave in care must be distracted, appeased, but not confronted (and we parents would not want carers to take such firm disciplinary action). It's the same with affection – it has to be diluted. Nap time is spent on a mat, not in an armchair in the arms of a loving relative. If carers wanted to give this amount of affection (and they often do) they would not have the time.

A child will often attract far more notice in childcare if they present a problem. Aggressive children, or very upset children, get attended to. Well-behaved children may be invisible. Childcarers have told us of the labelling syndrome, by which a child develops in the first few days an identity as a 'problem child', when it may just have been having a tough time settling in. The 'word' on who is being 'a problem' is passed on – from shift to shift and then from year to year. This reputation can follow a child right through to school.

A parent approaches their own child in a totally different way to the way they approach anyone else's. We talked to one crèche director who sends her own child to another crèche, because she felt it would be unfair to have him around when she is in her professional role. Another had the opposite policy – she wouldn't dream of having her child away from her.

We parents are intensely interested in our own child. Notice how you bore your friends with every detail of your child's progress. Look at it from the child's point of view. Might it not matter to a child to spend its first two or three years among people who adore it, who long to see it learn and grow, and have a personal investment and pride in it? Although a paid worker may genuinely care about children's wellbeing and advancement, the best they can ever feel is to be fond of your child, and be tender towards it in a general sort of way. What they have to offer will never equal a parent's investment and intensity.

QUALITY CARE IS STILL JUST CARE

The most overused word in the childcare debate is 'quality'. Nobody is happy with the idea of bleak, overcrowded childcare centres with cold and cruel staff. But 'quality' care is usually proposed as being equal to (or even, it is implied, better than) the care a parent can provide.

Care isn't love

The real question has to be whether children receive continuity of care, from individuals who have a long-term relationship with them, whom they come to trust and love.

Love is at the heart of the whole matter. It might be possible to improve the intimate connection children make with staff by addressing issues like staff rostering, size of groups, whether carers move through with the same group, and how many different adults are supposed to interact with a child during their time in care.

The debate about quality generally centres on training of staff, facilities, nutrition and educational programmes. All these are important, but they sidestep the question of quality relationships. Spending one's early childhood in the care of twenty or thirty different individuals (even in the best of settings) is still a very odd kind of childhood.

The use of the word 'childcare' is a great piece of marketing. We have to ask: is childcare actually just 'minding' children, or 'educating' them, or is it 'raising' them? If you spend eight or nine hours a day of infancy and toddlerhood in a crèche, then these people are surely raising you. Yet no one in the childcare industry is proposing that professionals take over the primary role of the parents. It has somehow been assumed that parents will still provide all that is needed, even though parent–child contact time has shrunk, and shrunk, and shrunk. The development of intimacy skills in a child in care may not be happening at all. The child as a person may be falling through the cracks.

Childcare academics have high aims, but the reality is often different. Childcare students and new workers we interviewed often spoke of the huge gap between their college or university ideals of 'individualized programmes' and 'one to one interaction', and the reality of life in a busy centre. Childcare is a highly stressed occupation – health problems, rapid turnover and total burnout in workers and directors are very common.

In order of preference, parents' first choice is family or close friends. The second choice – registered childminder – is also a more natural arrangement, where a mother at home cares for several other people's children, in a carefully regulated scheme that assures quality and safety. Childcare centres cater for the more mobile city-dwelling parents who need long day care beyond the ability of family or friends to provide, and need a more commercial arrangement. **What is the big picture?**

Childcare can begin very young. It's not unusual for career parents in capital cities to place their babies in long day care at six or twelve weeks of age (sometimes from 7.30 a.m. to 6.00 p.m. for five days a week). Centre directors experience pressure to take babies at weekends too. Once these children reach school age, they will experience the daily two-step from home to before-school care, then school, then after-school care, then home.

Despite the demand, childcare is highly undervalued. Workers are abysmally underpaid. Many more mothers would choose to stay home with their own children and be registered childminders if the financial rewards were better. We just don't put enough value on children. In most British cities, it costs more to park your car than to park your kids.

The real problem – the motherhood ghetto There are two things which drive mothers back to work when they would rather be at home.

One is economic dependency. Depending on another person's income can make the parent at home feel vulnerable and depressed. The non-earning partner can be made to feel that her work is worthless since she is 'just caring for kids'.

Another reason is the fear of 'going up the wall' – being with small children for company all day. This is a real problem, but not exactly a child's fault. The problem lies in the whole way we live. Our suburbs and apartment blocks may look pleasant enough, but are often very lonely places. We live surrounded by strangers, and the only social life is a trip to the supermarket. It's possible, through neighbourhood houses, playgroups, churches, swimming clubs and other organizations, to become more connected, and to bring about social change. But to do this, a person needs to be fairly confident and socially skilled.

It could be argued that Ethiopian farmers or Calcutta slum dwellers have a better life than Westerners in terms of social support and sheer friendliness of daily living.

Revitalizing the suburbs

If more parents were at home in the daytime, then things in the suburbs would soon change. You can already see this happening – playgroups, neighbourhood houses, and many other formal and informal networks of women and men are developing. Some of these will be oriented around children, others will be purely for self-development, or action groups for important issues like the environment, or more resources for families.

As men choose to be more family focused, and as more people work at home (thanks to computers) or work shorter hours, suburbs may change from deserted dormitories into lively and safer places where life goes on at its best.

Should parents be paid?

In many parts of the world, a radical idea is being discussed which has the potential to dramatically improve family life. The idea is that if we really value children, if we really want to 'save the family' we should pay a wage to mothers or fathers who choose to care for their own young children, full-time, at home.

Once, not long ago, families could live on the wage packet brought home by one person. The 1950s were not prosperous times, yet supporting a family was relatively easy. Today, fifty years later, many families need two incomes to survive. What has gone wrong ?

The two full-time income family is now very common, and often a necessity. But it is not a happy situation. In every street of every city and town in Britain, families are cracking up under the strain of both working and raising kids. You can see this amongst your friends, your neighbours, perhaps in your own house. Two-income families tell of horrendously stressed lifestyles, rushing to childcare each day, commuting across town, trying to snatch sleep each night, barely earning enough to offset the costs of childminding, transport and so on, then guiltily spending the money on making it up to the kids for not being there for them. Marriages are breaking down needlessly through sheer lack of time to build relationships. Health is being damaged through overwork, kids are being neglected and mistreated, and many teenagers are left to their own devices far too much. Serious problems, such as drug abuse, crime and early pregnancy, have all been found in studies to correlate with one reliable factor – lack of parental time and involvement.

It's not just our own kids. Parents used to give more time to running scout troops, helping at school, coaching children's sport, caring for elderly relatives: just being a community. Now it's all we can do to just make a living, feed the kids, get to sleep and go to work again the next day.

Is Life Just Earn and Spend? The economic view of life that governments seem to have taken – whether New Labour or Old Conservative – is that we are here in this life to earn and spend. If you are not in a job, you are not a full member of society. Making Spice Girl dolls on a production line is seen as a valuable economic activity, but raising a child with care and skill is not. Yet the value of the work that is done at home is greater in real financial terms than all our mining, agriculture and manufacturing productivity put together.

I spoke about this to a Family Committee of MPs at the House of Commons in May 1998, and challenged the MPs present about whether they really valued parenting.

For instance, the Government has put a lot of pressure lately on single mothers to return to the workforce. This makes sense if they are not to be welfare dependent. But surely this could wait until their children are at least of school age. Several MPs tried to reassure me that they did not wish to devalue the role of mothers, but the reality, as some of the community representatives present pointed out, is that single mothers feel acutely insecure.

So the bottom line is this. Parents carry out an enormously valuable function. It just doesn't show up in financial terms except in a hidden way – ten years later, when we either have happy, healthy and contributing citizens, or rising crime, breakdown, misery and a horrific underclass that grows in size every year.

Millions of people don't have any work. And millions have too much work. Many people with jobs now work fifty- to sixty-hour weeks just to hold onto them. We should be smart enough to share work more, to flow flexibly between full- and part-time work, men and women swapping and sharing as our life cycle dictates.

The kind of economy we have now wants women, and not men. All through the eighties and nineties, jobs in manufacturing began disappearing, while demand for women in lowpaid service jobs soared. The result is a 'women's work ghetto' that tears young mothers in half as they try to balance children and income earning, in jobs which are often menial and boring.

The Right to Parent

Women and men have an equal right to work. But what about the right of mothers or fathers of young children NOT to work? At the moment, many women do not have this choice. (Working fathers have long been deprived of real time with their children.) Once women had to fight for the right to a career. It seems we now have to fight for the right to parent our own children.

How Would Parent Pay Work?

What would be the effect of paying a weekly grant to people who stay at home to raise their young children – say up to school age ?

The first thing would be to remove sexism. The choice of who goes to work and who stays at home should be an individual choice of the couple. A dad may well be the one who prefers to be the at-home parent. Stay-home fathers are a growing phenomenon worldwide.

A high proportion of mothers currently in full-time jobs (some studies put it around 60%) would prefer not to work while their children are very young, but cannot afford to stop working. A parent pay system would mean this group would begin vacating jobs, depending on the level of pay, and those jobs would be available to others currently unemployed.

This is not an argument for chaining women to the home. Both men and women need the stimulation, participation and rewards that work brings. However, going out to work must be a real choice. Women often have to work at unfulfilling, menial, deadend jobs while their little children are cared for by strangers at great expense, and with a lot of heartache, inconvenience and stress. (Sometimes they take these jobs because they are the only jobs that allow flexibility of hours.)

Some practicalities would be involved. Families would nominate who is the 'at home' parent, and that person would be personally entitled to parent pay. If they took part-time work, then parent pay would be reduced. To prevent dependency (or people having dozens of babies to cash in!) parent pay would NOT be based on the number of children. And it would cease once a child started school.

We can never actually reimburse the effort of parenthood. If carried out by paid professionals, parenting would cost over £50,000 per year per child. Yet even small grants to at home parents begin to make an impact, and it would be a matter of adjusting this amount to find where it began to make a difference.

Other countries have made moves in this direction. In Sweden the Government pays you 90% of your prebirth salary for up to 18 months from birth, for whichever parent leaves the workforce to care for the baby. Other countries use tax breaks and other means to help parents be parents.

Parent pay is very much a feminist cause. It's one of the most ingrained aspects of sexism to value the work of a male executive or a tycoon who might produce little of value, while devaluing the enormously positive work that is done in the home and the community by people (usually women) who are paid nothing.

Parent pay, even at a modest level, is a step towards a different kind of society, where the economy serves the people, and not the other way around. It is as fundamental and as powerful as that. Please think about it and talk it over with others. Sometimes we have to ask the big questions and get our society going in a better direction, and this is one of those times.

CONFLICTING VIEWS –
THE EXPERTS SLUG IT OUT

'Poor quality care in these years can sometimes harm young children. Leaving babies and toddlers unattended and unoccupied for long periods, inappropriate discipline, lack of a good planned program or even leaving a distressed child uncomforted can make childcare an unhappy experience for parents and children alike.'
Labour Policy Statement, 1993 Federal election, Australia.

'I've never advised mothers who wanted a career not to pursue it, but I think it's very cruel for mothers who would rather stay at home to have to turn their kids over to someone else. If a mother wants to stay home with her baby, the Government should subsidise her, as in most other western countries.'
Benjamin Spock, the *Mercury*, Hobart, November 1992.

'From my experience, childcare (if carefully chosen) is not just good for children, they thrive on it! They benefit from a rich, stimulating environment away from the narrowness of an exclusive relationship with one parent. They have a larger view of the world and learn to share and cooperate with one another. They spend time with adults who enjoy being with them, and zoom in on their needs day after day. They are creative, self reliant and, I suspect, appreciate their parents a little more because their time together is so special.'
Rosemary Lever, *Such Sweet Sorrow*.

'Quality care is hard to come by, and even if you are one of the lucky ones, once your children are in care your life will entail a daily round of juggling childcare pickups and daily duties. If you're anything like me you will also have to live with a mixture of feelings and impossible contradictions, swinging between joy, happiness, or gloomy questioning about whether the care you have chosen is suitable, whether the children are happy, whether they're getting enough time and attention from you.'
Rosemary Lever, *Such Sweet Sorrow*.

'The fact is that the children of good, working parents are just as happy and turn out equally well as those of parents who don't work. It is not quantity of time you spend with your child that counts, it is the quality.'

Christopher Green, *Toddler Taming.*

'Regular absences can be damaging for children under three. Only from ages three to six, can most children profit from a whole day in high quality group care. But even then, there is a consensus among preschool educators that the benefits of a good preschool program diminish or are even cancelled when the school day is prolonged to six hours or beyond.'

Selma Fraiberg, child psychoanalyst, quoted by Karl Zinsmeister in 'Hard Truths about Day Care', *Readers Digest*, January 1989.

' . . . infants in day care are more likely to develop insecure attachments to their mothers, withdrawal from their mothers, and were more likely to hit, kick, threaten and argue, than those who were not in day care or started later.'

'Children with a record of early non-parental care show more serious aggression, less cooperation, less tolerance of frustration, more misbehaviour, and at times social withdrawal.'

Karl Zinsmeister, 'Hard Truths about Day Care', *Readers Digest*, January 1989.

' . . . the point is that day care was introduced for the adult's benefit and investigations into whether or not it is helpful or damaging for the child come later. Day care is about adult economics, adult behaviour, and adult desires.'

Bob Mullen, *Are Mothers Really Necessary?*

'Bruner (1980) concludes that in its present form, childminding creates problems for at least a third of the children in such care, and for possibly as many as half.'

Bob Mullen, *Are Mothers Really Necessary?*

'Sheila Kitzinger notes that the social context of childbearing has become negative and rejecting – childbearing is an interruption of people's "real" lives. Kirtzinger adds that this particular ethos which downgrades motherhood and childrearing, attributes to those mothers who find motherhood satisfying a mindless, sentimental form of idiocy. Kitzinger believes that in the women's movement, whatever that might be, there is an ambiguous approach to motherhood.'

Bob Mullen, *Are Mothers Really Necessary?*

'First time parents are often unprepared for the intensity of love they have for their children. One mother I met recently described it as being "metamorphosed". She held a senior position in a large banking firm and had committed herself whilst pregnant to an early return date. The day we met she marvelled about how changed she felt by the birth of her child, how privileged, how much more love she had to give and how painful it was even to contemplate leaving her precious baby with anyone else.'

Rosemary Lever, *Such Sweet Sorrow.*

The choices we make about childcare should be based firstly on the developmental needs of our child.

Recommendations

As mentioned earlier in this chapter, there are no conclusive research results that set down what is right for every child. We parents have to use our own good sense. The following are guidelines I recommend.

BY AGE

In your child's first year, do not use institutional childcare at all.

Organize for your baby to be with one of you all the time, except for occasional breaks – days off or evenings out, when you have a trusted and familiar babysitter.

If you are using institutional childcare, we suggest you consider these guidelines:

When the child is one – up to one short day per week, for example, 10 a.m. to 3 p.m.

When the child is two – up to two short days per week.

When the child is three – up to three short days or half-days a week.

When the child is four – up to four short days or half-days a week.

Your decisions should always be based on the needs of the individual child, and through monitoring its reactions from day to day.

99

BY TYPE OF CARE

In order of preference, we believe the best source of childcare for your child under the age of three would be:

✳✳✳ *Close relative or friend* whom you trust and who loves your child.

✳✳ A trustworthy and *friendly family day carer*, whom you know personally.*

✳ A *quality childcare centre*, with stable staff whom you get to know and feel comfortable with.

*If you cannot find a family day carer you are really comfortable with, then a childcare centre is probably better.

For children three years and older, good childcare centres can come into their own. At this age, the benefits of social interaction, planned activities, playing space and equipment, and professionally trained and motivated staff are a major bonus.

BY YOUR CIRCUMSTANCES

As well as the needs of the child, the needs of the family unit must be weighed in – because the child will suffer anyway if, for instance, a parent becomes sick, or a marriage breaks down, or a family cannot keep its home through lack of income.

If childcare is truly good for your family, it will be filling the following criteria:

1. It helps your survival – for instance, when you need to work to provide for material needs.

2. It gives you time to care adequately for other children, for example a new baby or a sick child.

3. It provides things for your child that you can't provide – resources (if poor), stimulation (if limited at home), friends (if isolated or an only child).

4. It meets your standards on discipline, respect for the child's being, and safety.

5. It builds long-term relationships – carers become your friends, and friends of your child.

6. It is a setting where you feel welcome to drop in at any time, spend the day with your child, make special requests or let them know of concerns, without ever feeling you are a bother.

By balancing a child's needs, and one's changing family situation, informed choices can be made which may work out very well.
Good luck!

Too, too, too

Childcare is here to stay. What we have to guard against is childcare overuse. Our standards have somehow slipped. We have been sucked in by economic rationalism, and stopped listening to our own hearts.

The result – children are being put into care too young, for too long hours, too many days a week.

The inadequate provision of childcare means that parents are having to use too many different forms of care, even in the same day, to meet their needs.

Childcare workers are paid too little, and there are too many children. Centre-based care is too unnatural and mechanistic a form of looking after young children, too factory-like for comfort.

In the future, there will be a place for childcare, but it will be a smaller place than it now occupies. While everyone talks about the need for more childcare places and bemoans the waiting lists, it may be that one day there will be less demand for it, and places will be abundant for those who really need it. Little babies and toddlers will mainly be cared for once again where they have been for millennia – by their parents, neighbours and family members, in the arms and in the homes of those who love them.

IS THIS THE PERFECT WAY TO LIVE?

On a wooded suburban ridge overlooking Hobart's harbour, a cluster of houses stands out only slightly from the conventional houses close by. They have warm, earthy colours, detailed woodwork in Tasmanian timbers. More noticeably, they have no road, only landscaped pathways and discreet parking bays at the edge of the three-acre site.

This is the Cascade Cohouse – a form of living for people of all ages that has been highly successful in northern Europe, and is now gaining a foothold in Australia. For a young family that has to live in the city, this may well be the perfect way to live.

The setup

Cascade Cohouse consists of fifteen dwellings which run along a hillside, curving at one end to face a larger common building which everyone shares the use of.

A large, attractive 'village square' is at the centre and a pedestrian pathway curves amidst gardens and terraces. On completion of the Cohouse, thirty to forty people will live here. They will each own their own freehold. Each dwelling fronts on to common pedestrian space, but has a private back garden.

Best of all, all occupants will share in the large common building with dining room for forty people, children's playroom, well-equipped workshop, meditation spaces, office space and kitchens. Occupants may interact and join with other people on a daily basis, or be entirely private since the houses are quite self-contained.

This isn't a commune yet it is a real community. One of the nicest parts of Cohouse living is that a shared evening meal system exists. Each adult member is rostered to cook a meal for the community from time to time. At present that means once every eight weeks – it's your turn! Eventually these meals will be held four evenings a week. For a young working father or mother, this means that instead of arriving home from work and scraping a meal together for the family, one can often simply stroll over to the Commonhouse for a delicious prepared dinner.

A safe place for children to grow

Ian and Jane, two young scientists who were founding members of the Cohouse, explained how the Cohouse situation was ideal for them as parents of a two-year-old child. They could, if they wished, go out two or three nights a week and have excellent childminding available. Their little girl could walk to the houses of her young friends or older members of the Cohouse who enjoyed having young ones around. Since this was a group of people who knew each other and chose to live in community, the feeling of trust and companionship was everywhere.

Young mothers or fathers at home during the day had company for a chat simply by strolling outside or going to the Commonhouse. There was a flat for visitors of residents.

Older people felt secure and never lonely – although privacy was respected and designed into the buildings.

Inexpensive living

Costwise, the residents at Cascade Cohouse found that they could build a very attractive dwelling of ten to twelve squares for around £35,000. Purchasing the freehold and common ownership of facilities – including the thirty square Commonhouse – cost an additional £16,000 or so. This included all hidden costs such as service connection and stamp duty (which normally add over £4,000 to the cost of a suburban block).

Cohouses provide many qualities in living that simply could not be bought – companionship, safety, meals, low travel costs, solar design and all kinds of sharing potential. Some cohouses in Europe have shared ownership in holiday homes and yachts at the coast, and have their own swimming pool or sauna.

5

Raising boys

It's time that we plan
for a new kind of man ...

If you have a daughter, then things are looking up for her. Because of the gains women have struggled for and won in the last few decades, your daughter will have as much chance of being a doctor as of being a nurse, a boss as a secretary. She will have the right to equal pay, the right to leave a violent husband, and the means to do so. Nobody will own her.

But there is still a long way to go. Your daughter will not have the freedom to walk about at night. In her life she will meet all kinds of barriers caused by men's inner insecurities. She may have trouble finding a man to settle down with who is as emotionally healthy as she is. Clearly, in the progress we are making through feminism, there's a missing step – something has still got to happen with *men* to bring them along on the journey to freedom that women are making. We can make a big difference if we start early, with boys.

Giving boys a positive self-image

Think about the present situation of boys. If you hear on the radio about a gang of youths causing a fight, you're pretty sure it will be boys, not girls. When we talk about teenage suicide, in four out of five cases we mean boys. The driver of a crashed car, the cause of a high-speed chase, the problem child in the classroom or playground, the burglar, the serial killer, the corporate criminal, the dictator – why is it almost always a bloke?

> Boys have five times as many learning problems, ten times as much problem behaviour at school. As adults they will have four times the vehicle accident rate, and nine times the imprisonment rate.

If you have boy children, it isn't enough to let them grow up to be 'normal' – because normal for a man in today's world often means uptight, competitive and emotionally illiterate. It's time to start raising a 'new kind of man'.

This chapter is about realizing just how much more we can expect of boys if we are willing to expand our horizons for them.

The first step for us as parents is to get a clear idea of the kind of men we want our sons to be.

WHAT KIND OF MAN DO WE NEED?

A group of women is meeting in a weekend seminar on relationships. (In another room, the men who are their partners are also meeting together.) The leader asks the women to call out the qualities they look for in a man. After the quick rush of jokes, like 'Lots of money', and some unprintable comments, the women become more thoughtful. This is the list that they come up with.

Passionate

Self-reliant

Willing to share the work

Able to love deeply

Able to feel sorrow and admit fear, and not just turn everything into anger

Respectful to and supportive of women

Nurturing

Fearless and strong in good causes

Creative – not rigid or bound by convention

Respectful of others

Funny, but knows when to be serious

Stable, reliable (but not dull)

Sticks to a task, gets things done

Loving, but not gooey or dependent

Proud, but not egotistical

Safe and not violent

Able to dance and sing and enjoy the flowers

Not just a workaholic

Wild and free

Impulsive

Natural

These are what women look for in a man. It's a fairly safe bet that these are also what men are wanting to be in themselves.

So, when we are raising our sons, these can be some of the aims we have in mind. This awareness will guide our actions and help us know when to intervene in the smallest of everyday situations. When a boy is mean to his sister, or tickles her when she is clearly saying no – then as parents we come in very firmly and tell him not to do that. We would do just the same if she was mean to him. If he asks why, we tell him, 'I want you to grow up respecting people's bodies, and respecting your own too. When someone says *stop*, you *stop*.' You can see how important this is for a lifetime.

How the world treats boys There's something special and precious about boys – every parent of boys and girls notices that their natures are different. Boys tend to wear their feelings on their sleeves – often their passions are strong and they seem to have an urge to protect. They love heroism and action. Boys are loyal, stoic, and have a strong sense of justice. They are humorous, optimistic and up-front.

When I look at little boys, and then see how cheaply the world often treats them – how few of their special qualities are supported and nurtured – it makes me very sad.

There are two facts that sum up the situation of boys, and how much needs to be done to help them. First, the news released by UNICEF that Australia has the highest rate of youth suicide of any Western country, and that suicide is four times more common among our teenage boys than girls. The second is a figure reported some years ago – that fathers on average spend six minutes a day in interaction with their sons. Neither of these is much to be proud of, and the two are very probably linked. So it's timely that we look at what we can do to help boys turn out well.

We'll sum up what is needed, then go into each issue more fully.

1. Boys need fathers, or at least very good father-substitutes.

2. Fathers need help from other men to raise their sons.

3. Boys need to learn how to behave around girls – respecting them, being equal to them.

4. Boys need protection from being cheapened, hardened or debased by exposure to violence or banality. They need to see their sexuality as special, not cheap.

5. Boys need help to learn how to work and be self-sufficient around the house.

One hundred and fifty years ago, life was very different for men and boys. Almost all men worked in agriculture and home-based crafts and trades. So a boy grew up around his dad and the other men of the village or town; his uncles, cousins, grandparents, all took an interest in teaching him and befriending him. Then suddenly, when the industrial revolution began, whole villages were evicted and millions of people went to the cities and towns to work in the mills and mines. Mothers had the task of raising their sons, as the fathers were away at work six days a week for long hours. 'Wait till your father gets home!' became a common catchcry.

Where have all the fathers gone?

Losing the support of the village network, the family itself started to decline. A hundred years ago, an average family had 6.7 children. Few people we know want to go back to that! But families didn't just get smaller. They started to fall apart. Men left their wives, or never married in the first place. Soon a large number of children were being raised by single women. This trend has continued to the present day. Men are disappearing from the family picture. For instance, within a year of divorce, one-third of fathers have virtually disappeared from their children's lives.

A father can be around and still have 'disappeared' emotionally. Many working men are out of the home early, home late, and tired and ratty when they are at home. Little children may not see their father at all during the week – they are asleep when he leaves in the morning and again when he comes home at night. An unemployed father, if he gets his act together, has a better chance of being a good father than someone with a busy career.

Father absence hurts and damages little girls too, but it devastates little boys. Whether they show it by being aggressive, or compensate by being Mummy's little helper, a boy with no role models cannot learn how to be a man. Some psychologists believe it may take hours a day of male contact for a boy to learn how to be a man. If little David has a lady schoolteacher, lives with his mum, stays at Grandma's, and meets only Mum's women friends at home, he learns nothing about how to be a man. The absence of men in boys' lives is a big problem in our society.

What can you do if you're a single mum?

Women on their own can raise healthy sons. But, as I've learned from talking to lots of single mothers, it takes some special planning.

BEING FIRM, STAYING WARM

A single parent of either sex continually has to switch between and balance the firmlove and softlove sides of their nature. For a single mother, there will be a danger of losing the softness while trying to maintain the firmness you know your son needs. As a rule, women are less combative than men in their interaction style. You can see this in the way some men say things like, 'Not you again!', 'G'day you old bastard' and so on in their friendly greetings. So discipline generally comes more easily for a father than a mother. In fact, sometimes while a mother is trying to be firmer, her partner is trying to tone down his hardness and be more reasonable.

There are times when boys (mostly unconsciously) seek out a combative (friendly, safe, but very confronting) intensity to help them deal with their physical and hormonal surges. Get help – from friends, or professionally – if you feel you are losing the plot here. Especially with boys around fourteen years of age, a mother on her own needs to conserve energy and be well supported. It's especially important never to hit or strike out, or say hurtful kinds of things at these times.

FINDING THE RIGHT ROLE MODELS

You must actively look for role models for your son. Go down to the school and ask the headteacher for a good male teacher for your son next year. When choosing a sport or activity, choose it by looking at the kind of men that lead the activity. Is this the kind of man I want my son to be like? (That is what role model means. Looked at this way, the football coach or karate teacher could be great, or the pits!)

Sometimes an uncle or grandfather will take an interest if you ask them to do so – they may have been holding back because they were unsure if their help was welcome. You don't have to marry someone to get a good role model.

Be very, very choosy who your son spends time with. Paedophiles (men who sexually abuse children) often take advantage of boys with no fathers who are hungry for male attention. This isn't a rare problem – one in seven boys is abused at some time in his childhood. Always check out the men in your son's life.

SEND HIM TO HIS DAD

Unless your son's father is a dangerous or very irresponsible man, do your best to maintain contact between them. If you are separated or divorced,

WHY BOYS PLAY UP

Marcus is fourteen. He likes to go off in the evenings on his bike and muck around with his mates. One night, he's late for tea. When he comes in, his parents grumble and nag at him, but his father is only half-hearted about it. In the end, it's agreed that Marcus can come in when he pleases as long as he's in by dark, and that his tea will be left in the oven.

A few weeks later Marcus comes in really late, about nine o'clock. He says it wasn't really dark. His mother is upset, but his father says, 'Well, as long as he doesn't get into any serious trouble, and is in by ten. Boys like to have a bit of freedom.'

A few days later, Marcus is brought home by the police, who found him with CDs stolen from a nearby shopping centre. He is one of a group of mates to be charged with the offence.

Marcus's parents, especially his father, wanted to avoid trouble. But they missed the point that Marcus was breaking the rules to get noticed. When the rules were just bent to give him more scope, he had to break even bigger rules. Marcus's father is a senior manager, and has been away overseas a lot. An intelligent man, he will now make the connection and start to do some fathering. Marcus will be confronted about his behaviour, but, more importantly, his father will get more involved. A promotion involving extra travel will be knocked back so that he can be at home more of the time. It will cost him materially, but Marcus will stay out of jail.

Boys play up because they want to be 'met' by an equal investment of energy, preferably from fathers or father-substitutes. Boys whose fathers are uninvolved are especially drawn to 'hypermasculine' action figures, comics and games. They are trying to make up for the lack of masculinity in their real lives. Boys with involved fathers are noticeably quieter, more communicative and more settled. They achieve more at school, have fewer behaviour problems and are more often employed when they leave school.

Studies have found the incidence of drug addiction and alcoholism in boys is directly proportionate to the amount of time spent with parents. Adolescence is not a time to ignore your children.

but in good communication with your ex-husband, consider sending your son to live with his dad from the time the boy is about fourteen years old. Often boys get difficult to manage around fourteen. Without realizing it, they feel a strong need for male limit-setting. Women often fear taking this step – 'Oh, he wouldn't look after him properly!' Sometimes this is true. But more often fathers, if called upon to take on the parenting, will find that they have untapped nurturing and disciplining qualities. This arrangement can work out well for everyone.

Single parenting is heroic work. It's better to be a child in a single-parent home than in a bitterly unhappy intact family. The challenge for single parents is to supplement your own parenting with the right inputs for your kids.

What fathering really means

Many dads are great with their kids. However, many of us are completely at a loss regarding 'how to father'. Early in my children's lives I found it tempting to just leave parenting to my wife because she seemed so much better at it. Today, though, fathering is one of the biggest pleasures of my life.

Part of the reason for our incompetence is that we have a fathering vacuum – many men didn't have an involved father, just a strange man who shuffled newspapers in the corner of the lounge and grumbled occasionally. So we didn't have a deep pool of fathering behaviours to draw from.

Luckily I can say to you from experience, 'It ain't that hard' and 'Once you get started you'll soon get to like it.' Here are two or three good ways to start.

ROUGH AND TUMBLE

Boys love to wrestle, tickle, struggle, and play in vigorous, rough and tumble ways. This seems to be true at any age. Do this whenever you get the chance and have the energy. Choose a safe place. Give them a goal – to pin your arms, or escape from a bear hug.

There is more to it than just good fun – you can teach important lessons while you wrestle. By stopping if it gets too careless or dangerous, calming down and beginning again, you are teaching boys to handle and be calm with their strength. By always being good-humoured and not excessively competitive – letting them win, then winning again – you teach them that the fun is in the interaction, and to be good losers. Perhaps most importantly, play wrestling or 'rough and tough' is both a form of intimacy and a celebration of masculinity. (Though some daughters like it too, especially when they are little.)

My own father was not into hugging or outward displays of affection and, like many men of his generation, couldn't give a compliment to save his life. But he would always play wrestle with me, with my cousins and with nephews. Whenever we went visiting, he would be covered with kids. It was great!

DOING AND TEACHING

Robert Bly says, 'Even mean men are sweet when they teach.' Boys love to learn about the world of men. This might mean cars, computers, horses, birdwatching, football, fishing, woodwork – anything that they enjoy, and you enjoy showing them. (A clue – don't be perfectionist, or you'll just put them off. Share your enjoyment, not just your high standards.)

If you're a dad, you should be around your son and the rest of the family, talking and doing things, for at least an hour a day. If your work schedule prevents this, you might need to look seriously at your priorities. I would like to be more comforting about this, but being a career success today is almost incompatible with being a good father. Boys need to know you in all different moods and different activities.

SEEING YOU IN ACTION

If sons see you cooking meals, cleaning up and caring for younger kids, then they will also become more hard working around the home. Dads have to show they are more than just 'the good times man'. You can teach them by example how to be whole men. If they see you taking care of your body, treating other people well, expressing your emotions, standing up for what you believe in, then this will be more powerful than anything you might say. You might just have to become the kind of man you want your sons to be!

LISTEN UP!

One of the greatest life skills you can ever have is the ability – the willingness, really – to stop in the middle of an argument and listen to the other person's side of the story. It's a skill you could use at least five times a day . . .

One hot summer afternoon my son and I went down the gully to start the diesel pump. We do this once every summer to refill our dam with water. My son was four – a little young, you might say, but a necessary assistant. While I cranked the pump, his job was to flick the pressure switch at the critical moment for the pump to start.

The machine is huge and old, and we had several failed attempts. I was not in a good mood. Thistles stung my legs, and mosquitoes swirled about. My arm ached from turning the heavy crank. Then my assistant went on strike! He backed off around the dam! I could feel my anger rise. I prepared myself to bully him into doing as he was told. But he looked me squarely in the eyes, accusing almost, and I managed to catch myself. 'Why won't you help?' I asked, trying to make my voice sympathetic. 'It's too smoky. I can't breathe,' he said. Sure enough, a pall of diesel fumes hung around from our first attempts.

So we sat by the water for a few minutes, quietly relaxing before trying again. We chatted a little about the frogs and the insects. Then we started the pump first time!

It hasn't been the last time, and probably the experience gets more frequent as children get older and wiser. That moment of simple parental realization – 'They're right and I'm wrong.' And how important it is to listen.

LET YOUR SON MEET OTHER MEN

Involve your sons in activities with your friends so they can meet, learn from and get the approval of other men. Go on fathers-and-sons camping trips. Take your sons to work so that they see from time to time what you do with your life – where you fit into the big picture, what your ideals are. Let them see some of what you sacrifice, some of the hardship and endurance that your life involves.

Above all, be around for them. Have time to waste.

Boys need protection I was once waiting outside a primary school for a meeting at the end of the school day. A group of boys – grade three, eight-year-olds – were coming slowly out of the classroom. Seeing something wasn't quite right, I looked more closely. Several were wiping tears from their eyes. All looked pale, shocked. I discovered later from a parent that their teacher – a man – had just shown an '18' rated war video because it was Armistice Day. No discussion, no debriefing, no breaks – just ninety minutes of violence. Often men and boys get blamed for being unfeeling, aggressive, insensitive. But how do they become that way, except as a defence against what we assail them with?

You can do a lot to slow down the robbing of childhood from your sons (and daughters) by preventing them from watching endless violent cartoons or playing unimaginative games with war toys. (Kids do make guns from sticks, yes, but all you can do with a toy gun is pretend to kill.) Much war and violent play arises from watching violence, feeling frightened by it and so identifying with the war figures to get back a sense of power. Children in war zones play the most war games. Why should our sitting rooms resemble war zones? Why not have a home (and a TV environment) that brings in the feeling of a tropical island paradise, with nature, warmth, beauty and adventure?

It's the same with computers. Don't let your sons 'disappear' into banal computer games for hours on end – especially the kind with endless mazes and ladders – which are addictive and teach nothing but a twitchy finger.

Provide more active, sociable and natural kinds of activity. Spend time with your sons rather than buying things for them. Value and compliment their ability with little children, and their sensitivity to feelings and fairness. Have a pet that they can be active with. Do this and you will see the natural lovingness come out in your boys.

Boys need help in learning to relate

One good thing that a mother or father of boys can do is to teach them to get along with the opposite sex, and help them to talk to and cooperate with girls. Insist they treat girls with respect and care. When they become teenagers, don't let them put pictures from girlie magazines on their walls. Most boys are interested in women's bodies, but you can help to keep sex and sexuality special and not just sleazy and cheap.

Teach your son to respect women

As a dad, you do this in two ways – by showing respect to women yourself, and by coming down hard on any disrespect that is shown by a son to his mother. An old saying, 'Don't speak to your mother like that', sets the scene for an important moment in family life. It should only need to be said once.

As a mum, calmly and clearly demand respect. Mediate with your son and his sisters so that they are able to express their feelings, and to learn respectful problem-solving instead of name-calling and intimidation. Be even-handed. Boys have feelings – remember this yourself, and teach your daughters this. If boys are treated as though they have no feelings, then they become unfeeling to protect themselves.

Ask your son about his feelings and acknowledge when he is sad or scared. Let him know when you have these feelings too. Avoid the emotional shutdown that makes men so stressed and depressed. Don't ever make fun of his soft side, especially his early love life. He can be strong and sensitive. They go together.

Help him learn housework skills

And praise those skills! By age nine, a son should be cooking a meal for the family each week and feeling proud of it. Even if it's only pasta and ready-made sauce to begin with, he can soon build up a creditable menu. Help him to get started in the kitchen. Most boys will gain enjoyment from making such a contribution.

Make it routine that he picks up after himself, learns to do laundry and to mend. If he doesn't, don't nag – just double his workload for that day. The common response from Supermum types is, 'But it's quicker if I do it for him – he just takes so long.' Yes, teaching takes time. But imagine having an eighteen-year-old who is as competent as you are, and who does as much housework as you do. Surely that's worth a little early investment!

In short

You are making a man. Think about the goals you have achieved, and those you still want to achieve. You could tick off on the list given by the women in the class at the start of this chapter (page 106). Which do you still want to work on?

At the very least, take time to have a dream about the kind of man you want your son to be. By making a commitment – 'My sons will turn into wonderful young men' – and starting to do the daily things that make this happen, you can, as a mother or father, achieve one of life's greatest satisfactions, and do the world a favour.

6

Raising daughters

Through her daughter, a mother sees her own life starting again. So a daughter has a powerful effect on her mother. And how a mother feels about her own life will deeply influence how she relates to her daughter.

Mothers and daughters

Mothers and daughters can have a closeness that is very beautiful. Or they can be an explosive combination! Mums and daughters usually understand each other deeply – sometimes to an extent that seems telepathic.

Mothers feel so strongly about their daughters, just as fathers do about their sons, because in a sense our children are a new version of us. They reflect back to us all our hopes, fears and feelings about our own lives. If you know this is going on, it helps. If you don't, it can lead to very weird behaviour! Things can get fiery, as our teenagers become especially sensitive to being loaded up with our expectations. Such situations have led more than one mother to tell me she prefers sons – they're so much simpler!

But it's worth it. Part of what makes raising a daughter so great an adventure for a mother is the potential for close friendship. In the meantime, though, your daughter is a little child needing your care. To care for her well, you may have to work free of some of your own hang-ups that could be getting in the way of clear parenting.

What do we mean by this? Let's expand.

Mothers see themselves in their daughters. For better or for worse, this generates all kinds of unconscious and conscious urges.

- They want their daughters to have more opportunities than they had.

- They want their daughters to stay close, but also to move out and have their own life.

- They want their daughters to get on with their dads.

- They want their daughters to find a man – as long as he's perfect!

- They want their daughters to have a life free from pain or trouble of any kind.

What do we mean by unconscious urges? Here's an example: A friend of mine had a mother who had known great poverty in her childhood. Her idea of good mothering was working long hours so that her daughters would be well provided for. The result was that her daughters had very little time with her, and were often placed in vulnerable situations while their mother was away at work. They would have been better off with less money and more protection.

Sometimes when our motivation is unconscious like this, we don't think through all the ramifications. The key to this is self-awareness. You listen to what comes out of your own mouth, and reflect on 'where you are coming from'. You realize that your daughters are not you, and give them room to make their own mistakes, find their own answers, define what they want.

The five ways of parenting Jean Illsley Clarke, in a superb book called *Growing up Again*, describes five different ways we can react to a child, which also tell us a great deal about ourselves. You can use these five styles as a diagnostic tool to find what is happening between you and your daughter. Most probably, you'll find confirmation that you are doing the right thing, which Clarke calls the 'assertively caring' style. The other styles can easily be recognized and help you to avoid doing harm.

When I first learned about these ideas (and this is talking as a dad) I found I was a real mixture of the different types. It was very helpful to think about.

Let's apply the five styles to a simple everyday situation: Merrilee, a little girl aged six, falls over while running in the park. She comes to her mother crying, with a badly scraped arm.

There are several ways her mother can react.

THE ABUSIVE STYLE

Her mother is busy talking to a friend. She turns and yells, 'Stop howling like that, or I'll really give you something to cry about.' As she does so, she yanks the little girl by the arm and takes her off home.

The message sent here is, 'You don't count. Your feelings don't matter. You're a nuisance to me.'

The child may feel deep pain and despair, or rage, or loneliness and withdrawal. But where is the mum coming from? If we're honest, many of us have felt overwhelmed at times, and reacted in a verbally abusive way. It's the reaction of a parent whose own needs are so unmet that she sees her daughter as a competitor.

This mother needs help of a nurturing, long-term kind so that she can refill her emotional fuel tank, heal her own childhood neglect, and in the meantime care for her daughter with more kindness.

THE CONDITIONAL STYLE

This mother says, 'Stop crying or I won't bandage your arm. What did you do that for anyway?' This kind of parent connects with the child by threats and conditions. The child has to meet with parental expectations, and only then will her needs be met. The message is, 'Don't believe you are loveable, you only get love if you earn it.'

The mother sends this message to her daughter because it's how she also views herself. This kind of parent is usually immaculate and uptight, setting super-high standards for herself and those around her. It's natural she will pass on the same messages to her child – especially if the child is the same sex child as herself.

The child will feel inadequate, never quite measuring up – since no one is ever perfect. The child is likely to grow up obsessive and over-achieving, perhaps anorexic, with a lot of trouble being close to other people. In adulthood, she may have a series of showy but short-lived marriages.

The conditional Mum needs to relax. She has to learn to find – and to give herself – love and approval just for being. She can learn to stop worrying so much about clothes, looks, money or achievement. She should find some friends who are happy slobs, and learn how it's done. In this way she can learn to accept that love is free and doesn't have to be earned. And then she can teach this to her children.

THE INDULGENT STYLE

Mummy rushes to the child before the little one has even had time to stand up. 'Oh, look at your arm. That really hurts, doesn't it? I'll bandage it now. We'll drive to the chemist and get some ointment. I'll make you a bed on the couch in front of the TV and I'll do your jobs for you.'

This sounds at first like a very kind mother. But listen to the deeper messages: 'You are a poor victim. You aren't capable – you need me to look after you.' At an even deeper level she is implying, 'We can't both meet our needs at the one time. I'll overindulge you, but you'll owe me.' Does this sound familiar to you?

The child in this relationship will have very mixed feelings. She will feel temporary comfort, but also a sense of obligation and resentment underlying it. She will feel weakened and confused by her parent's presence, rather than strengthened and encouraged. Jean Illsley Clarke calls this 'a sticky, patronising kind of love' which promotes dependency and a blurry sense of self.

The mother in this situation needs to build a stronger sense of self. Perhaps her childhood featured an alcoholic or otherwise needy parent who forced her to grow up too soon, and to be a caretaker instead of being loved. Perhaps one of her parents was also indulgent to mask inner neediness. She could benefit from reading books about codependency and getting good support in a healing kind of ongoing group.

THE NEGLECTFUL STYLE

Mum ignores the scrape. In fact, she's probably not even at the playground. The daughter is far from home, unsupervised, and nobody cares. This child may be fed and clothed, but her parents are uninvolved. She knows deep down that she dies or survives alone. If she has made it this far she will probably survive, but she is likely to be a very hard, lonely young person with all kinds of anger and disappointment hidden on the inside. She will possibly get into serious strife in an attempt to get cared for. As an adult she will have little ability to get close to others, unless help – in the form of an understanding teacher or youth worker – comes along soon.

Neglect is abuse, too – in some ways, one of the worst forms.

Before you get totally depressed, we'd better talk about the fifth kind of parenting style.

THE ASSERTIVELY CARING STYLE

This mother gives the little girl with the scraped arm a hug and loving care. She says things like, 'Your arm is scraped. I'm sorry you are hurt. How about I clean it up for you?' And then, 'How is it now?'

The child knows that she and her feelings matter. The mother is willing and available to help. Help is offered, not forced. The child feels comforted and relieved, secure, safe and loved.

There's more, too, in the big picture. This kind of mother lets her child grow in independence. If the child is only slightly hurt, or is somewhat older, the mother leaves her in charge of what happens. She says things like, 'Does it hurt? Are you able to go and wash it, or do you need some help?' This parent is available to give a hug, but is not too pushy. The message sent here is – 'I trust you to make your own judgements about what you need' (and, also, 'I don't need to be needed').

The assertively caring style is clearly the one to aim for.

Fathers with daughters

One of the things I've been struck by in my work is the great importance of fathers in shaping their daughters' self-esteem. I especially believe fathers should never put down their daughters' appearance even in 'fun'. Some men do this, perhaps out of some motive to 'tidy them up' or make them more presentable. The effect is usually the complete reverse.

127

There are many good things dads can do. They can give praise. They can also enjoy joking and laughing with their daughters, developing their skills in conversation and repartee. Be alert to the fact that girls change and go through very different phases, so that what was once a good topic to joke about can become an acutely sensitive one which is better left alone.

Fathers are a source of opposite-sex social practice. By conversing with their fathers about serious issues, by being admired for their mind as much as for their looks, girls learn to approach the opposite sex with the skills necessary to take the initiative and give as good as they get. They will never be bluffed or intimidated in male company. They will also have the confidence to pick and choose their partner rather than being passive wallflowers.

Building self-reliance in girls A father can build some good independence skills with his daughter – teaching her about cars, fixing things, woodworking, dealing with money, going camping. In this way he'll know she's safer out in the real world, and less dependent.

In a recent article, comedian Jean Kittson told how she grew up in a town where 'boys had cars, and girls had boyfriends'. She decided to get a car instead of a boyfriend, with her father's help, and escaped to the big smoke and a great career instead of being someone else's ornament!

Close but safe

Fathers who are clear about not sexually invading their daughters can still be affectionate and warm – they don't have to get all uptight. Sexual touch and affectionate touch are totally distinct.

Having a strong marriage also helps your daughter's development – she sees a man and woman relating respectfully. If a daughter knows that her parents are close, then she will feel safer around her father, since his needs for affection and sexual partnership are clearly being met. For this reason, be wary of taking your daughter's side against your partner – if you have a problem with your partner, then deal with it on a one-to-one basis.

Respect is a key element between the genders and you as a father can model it. If you respect your daughter (and her mother) then she will insist on other males doing the same. If you put her down, she may allow other males to do so too, thinking this is normal. Being respectful is usually as simple as extending normal courtesy. For example, you can respect your daughter's developing need for privacy by asking permission to enter her room when she is in there.

WHEN A CHILD IS DISABLED

In all of my books on family life, it's been a concern to me that I have nothing to say about parenting disabled children. Yet every time I go on tour, parents of babies with all kinds of difficulties come along for some possible assistance. Children with disabilities are part of the family and the community, and deserve to be included. As much as anyone else, they are a plus in all our lives.

I've always felt constrained through lack of personal experience. So I was delighted when I found a beautiful article in the Melbourne *Age* by a mother of a daughter who is severely intellectually disabled, and who can write about her child's life so far with real insight.

Mary Burbridge would be the first to say that her family life has had as many ups and downs as any other. However, it's clear to me that she has triumphed in all kinds of ways and that this would be the kind of message that other parents would like to hear. It is also an example of a very special relationship between a mother and her daughter.

My daughter, my for-ever baby

I have a darling baby. A patient, placid baby who nuzzles warmly into her sheepskin and gives me a sleepy smile when I come in. She sits up, bounces happily and reaches up for a cuddle. I lift her out of bed, and with both hands held she walks unsteadily to the bathroom to have her nappy changed.

She's at a delightful stage, liking to help with dressing and undressing, wanting to hold the spoon but making an awful mess, moving along on the furniture and pulling down whatever she can reach. She loves music – songs and rhymes sung to her, banging on the piano, clapping and finger games, and the neverending, pull-the-string music boxes. She enjoys being taken for walks on sunny days, snatching heads off flowers as we pass, and she would splash and laugh for ever in a warm bath or pool.

I've had my darling baby for nearly twenty years now, and, unless something happens, I guess I'll have her for another twenty years. She's been at the lovely seven- to nine-month stage for a long time, so I don't expect much change.

She still has a sweet baby face, innocent, unmarred by loss or disappointment or anger, and she still has her mass of blonde curls. But her hormones are those of a young woman – a plump, buxom, almost voluptuous young woman – and acne spoils her pretty face. Her hair, though darker now, is still her finest feature. How often I've had cause to be thankful for those lovely curls! People are usually uncomfortable, stuck for something to say, on first meeting my big baby, but they can always say, 'What beautiful hair!' And they do. It helps.

Others I know have a much harder lot with their 'for-ever' babies. Endless years with a fretful, crying child, every mealtime a turmoil of spitting resistance, all activity a cause of spasms and distress. Or a child with full mobility but never learning to heed 'no' or 'stop'; on the go all day every day, getting bigger and stronger with every year, being influenced by powerful adolescent hormones. And without the redeeming beautiful curls.

We met at a special playgroup, a group of young mothers coming to terms with the realization that our children were severely disabled. We talked through our guilt, our grief and disappointment, our anger, as we helped our babies to play, and we've kept in touch. Caring for a severely handicapped child is a big task, as is caring for a baby, but when supports are available it is not all-consuming.

We have had other children and been active in their lives, we've had part-time jobs while the children are in day care, our marriages have survived and we've had family holidays.

And we've become involved in 'the field', working to ensure that the best possible services and supports are available for our children, and for other disabled people and their carers.

School councils, accommodation committees, fund-raising and fetes, lobbying politicians, demonstrations and protests, and self-education – we've done it all, learning as we go. As our children reach nominal adulthood, there are further decisions to be made, battles to be won. We need to be sure that there are suitable day activities available for them when the school system is no longer an option, and that appropriate long-term accommodation will be provided when the time is right for them to leave our care.

For the most part, I've found people sensitive and helpful. Services and supports have been available when I have needed them, and the years have rolled by pretty smoothly.

But there have been jolts and hurts along the way. There was the ideologically pure occupational therapist, who removed my daughter's toys and music box from her wheelchair because they were 'age-inappropriate'. (I responded by tying a book, a chess set and a rock-music tape to her tray, and she banged and chewed them into oblivion.) Or the brutally honest doctor at the children's hospital who said, when I rushed her to casualty with croup, 'I can admit her if you like, but she'd be better off at home. Children like that don't get the best treatment here'. And the bastard who publicly queried my use of a disabled parking sticker (before the rules changed).

Dilemmas arise in the decisions I need to make on my daughter's behalf. As she reached puberty, I was offered, and accepted with misgivings, a hormone injection to stop her having periods. I think I secretly hoped it would stop her body from maturing: that I would be able to pretend for ever that she was still a child. But it didn't, and after a year or so I stopped the injections.

'Why should she wear a bra?' I wondered, until physical size provided an obvious answer. 'What clothes should she wear?' I tend to dress her for her comfort and my convenience, but is this undermining her dignity as a young adult, denigrating her worth as a person? Should I dress her in the sort of things her sister wears; make an outlandish fashion statement on her behalf? What would she choose for herself if she could choose, and does it matter, since she has no concept of fashion or dignity? (These are issues one is made uncomfortably aware of, when working in the broader disability field.)

In deciding to seek an operation to stop her menstruating, was I motivated by her best interests or mine? (The social welfare authorities accepted that it would be in her best interests. Such important decisions are not made by carers alone.)

In years past, children such as ours would very likely have been placed in institutions at an early age. Parents of babies with much lesser disabilities were often advised not to take them home. 'Put her in a home and forget you ever had her,' they were told. And many did.

Recently I spent some time at a large institution, holding meetings with disabled people, their parents and their carers, and I observed a most amazing and moving phenomenon. The residents were in their thirties and had lived in the institution for more than twenty years. The staff were in daily contact with them and met all their physical needs. The parents visited from time to time. Yet, repeatedly, I was struck by the strength and durability of the emotional bond they had with their parents.

They couldn't get close enough, couldn't take their eyes off them, couldn't bear for the parent's attention to be anywhere but on them. An ungainly, nonverbal woman manoeuvred laboriously along the table and sat on her father's knee, pressing her face to his. I felt so sad that these people had not been offered the encouragement and support to keep their child at home for longer; to make the most of the love that was so obviously shared.

These days, fewer disabled children are born. Preventive immunization, genetic counselling and improved obstetric care have contributed to this. Special tests early in pregnancy can identify many malformations or abnormalities, and parents can choose to have the pregnancy terminated. While very few people would choose to bring a severely disabled child into the world if they could avoid it, the implications of this newly acquired capacity to engineer a largely disability-free society need to be examined.

What message does it give to disabled members of our community about their worth, their right to exist and be supported? Will society refuse support for those families who knowingly give birth to a disabled child? Will even minor defects be eliminated, until only perfection is tolerated? And what will this mean for those whose disabilities or deformities could not be predicted, or are acquired after birth?

A friend of mine recently had tests early in her pregnancy, because in her first pregnancy the baby had been found to have a severe foetal defect, necessitating termination, and there was a chance this could recur. She was told these tests showed a different problem, Down's syndrome, and that arrangements had been made for her to have a termination two days later.

She was offered no counselling about what having a child with Down's syndrome would mean, or what factors she would need to consider in making her decision. It was not even appreciated that she had a decision to make! In fact, it was a very difficult decision for her, and only after a lot of heartbreak did she accept that she really could not manage a disabled child in her situation. The attitude to disability shown by her doctors is a little disturbing.

So. What am I saying in all this? There will always be children born with disabilities. And if it happens to you, it's not the end of the world – for you or your baby. No one can predict with certainty what path any child's development will follow. Or what sort of life he or she will be able to lead.

It will not be the life you dreamt about when you were expecting your baby, but it is his or her life. Having a disabled child makes you think about life: what it's for; what's important. And your ideas change quite a lot.

Your life won't be the one you were dreaming about either, but it will be a full life, a rich life. And it could have a lot of joy.

7

Family liberation

At the end of a book that has covered so much ground, I want to share a vision with you. It involves the big picture beyond our homes, but it applies to everything that happens within them. Something new is starting to happen in the world of the family – something that means we can begin to change the world we live in, without leaving our own neighbourhoods to do it.

Time for change Parents have never had a real political voice – perhaps we're just too busy with little children to find the energy. It's as much as some of us can manage to crawl down to a voting booth every five years. But all this is starting to change at express-train speed.

PARENTS ARE ANGRY

Having left the care of our world to politicians and technocrats, what have we ended up with?

Our world is so *polluted* that we sustain genetic damage, and have soaring rates of miscarriage and infertility. Asthma, a problem highly related to air quality, is now a problem for one in every five British children. Likewise with allergies and reactions to the chemical environment. Even the sunshine has become a danger.

Our world is *violent* because of inequity, and crushed families, and a media that promotes violence as a way of life.

Our *economy* is unable to give meaningful or satisfying employment to our men or our teenagers, but it will employ our young mothers, as long as they don't mind what kind of work they do or how poorly they are paid.

When it comes to politics – the 'leadership' of our country – we want a better choice.

When it comes to politics, people are wanting a new priority – that puts people and community first and is not ruled by economic rationalism, yuppie values or earning power as the only measure of human worth.

A POSITIVE NEW ALLIANCE

When there is so little choice and so much frustration, then a new alternative always emerges. In this case, it draws support (surprisingly) from both sides of the philosophical fence. An amazing new alliance is appearing in your neighbourhood – between stereotyped groups such as the alternative lifestyle, high-tech, soft green people, and the right-wing, family-oriented, Christian traditionalists.

This is leading to all kinds of beautiful break-outs from the old stereotypes. When I give lecture tours around Australia, I am meeting at the same gatherings highly responsible, monogamous and hard-working 'hippies' – side by side with straight-backed churchgoers who hug their children, renounce smacking, belong to Amnesty International and boycott Nestlé!

I believe that more and more parents are working positively towards a world that embraces serenity, compassion, free-spiritedness and happiness.

The way forward

In fact, I don't think it is too optimistic to say that a kind of parent power is emerging. It will include and be merged with the green movement, because parents and children are natural environmentalists. It will embrace both feminism and the men's movement, because parents want a good future for both boys and girls, and it will support moves to advance gender relationships. It will make a huge difference to the shape of the twenty-first century.

So, to end this book, here is a suggested manifesto.

A STATEMENT OF BELIEFS TO GUIDE ACTIONS IN FAMILY LIBERATION

- Nothing is more important than raising healthy, happy children.

- No one can or should raise children alone. We all need each other's help.

- In particular we need a society that takes parents' needs very seriously, and funds those needs, in return for the gift we give back of healthy, contributing adults.

- The best way to make children safe is to take more care of parents.

- The best way to deprogramme our overscheduled children is to deprogramme ourselves.

- Parents are responsible to their children – for not smoking around them, for fastening their seat belts, for protecting them from abuse. Kids are not property.

- We must work at allowing children to hang on to childhood as long as possible.

- We must work to increase the positive contact between children and adults. This means abandoning smacking, and fighting sexual abuse, but it also means showing people better ways of connecting with their kids.

- We have to become active mentors to younger people, helping young parents, caring for other people's children, so as to spread the load of raising our young from the overburdened nuclear family into something we haven't had for a long time – real community.

- We have to have family-friendly workplaces, guaranteed by legislation, where fathers and mothers can fit work around their families' needs, instead of having to choose between career and family.

- The concept of family must be broadened to include everyone – single, gay, childless, divorced, elderly, criminal, refugee, businessman, homeless teenager.

We have to put our arms around everyone and say, 'Welcome home!'

Resources

The Mother and Baby Book by Shaaron Biddulph (available from Parent Network; tel. 0171 735 1214) is a beautiful and detailed guide to the craft of loving and educating babies through to preschool age. It is a book that only a woman could write.

Children's Relaxation Tape by Madhu Lilley is one of the most beautiful aids for children to relaxing and falling asleep with positive and strengthening imagery. Of the many beneficial relaxation tapes, this simple one is the favourite of our children. Available from Parent Network, tel. as above.

Parents and *Practical Parenting* magazines, as well as the publications of the National Childbirth Trust and National Breastfeeding Alliance, all have good, critical and consumer conscious news and views on parenthood and are good value.

The most progressive and non-commercial publication in the world that we have found is *Mothering* magazine, available from PO Box 532 Mt Morris, Illinois 61054, USA. We find this a great source of inspiration.

On the subjects of fathering and of raising boys, Steve's book *Manhood* is published by Hawthorne Press. On marriage and couple relationships, Steve and Shaaron's book, *The Making of Love*, is available from Parent Network; tel. as above.

Acknowledgements

I am profoundly indebted to Shaaron Biddulph for her skill with children, and the balance she brings to my masculine way of writing. Shaaron conceived of the sections on childcare damage and 'our home is a no smacking zone'. She refined the use of 'stand and think' and 'dealing' as applied to young children, and has taught these ideas to hundreds of parents. Our son and daughter learned with us. And, as with every family, hundreds of people helped.

Many thanks to Paul Stanish for drawing the cartoons, and Steve Miller for the beautiful cover design. And especial thanks to Wanda Whiteley, Charlotte Ridings, Paul Redhead and Megan Slyfield at Thorsons UK for believing in our books and bringing them to that sceptred isle.

Thanks to Boxtree Limited for permission to quote from *Are Mothers Really Necessary?* by Bob Mullen; Rosie Lever for permission to quote from *Such Sweet Sorrow*; Christopher Green for permission to quote from *Toddler Taming*; *Readers Digest* magazine for permission to quote from Karl Zinmeister's article, 'Hard Truths about Day Care'; the Australian Institute of Family Studies, especially Gay Ochiltree for her book, *Children in Australian Families*; the Melbourne *Age* and Mary Burbridge for permission to use in full her article, 'My Daughter, My Forever Baby'; the Melbourne *Age* for permission to use an excerpt from their editorial on parent pay; the *Mercury*, Hobart, for permission to reproduce the Benjamin Spock quote and the material on working mothers; the library staff at the Institute for Early Childhood Development at Kew, Melbourne, for their help and research facilities.

Raising Boys

Steve Biddulph

Everyone who has boys today is concerned for them. Everywhere we look, boys are having trouble with their lives. Parents want to understand better what makes boys tick, and how to help them be happy, loving and capable.

In *Raising Boys*, Steve Biddulph looks at the most important issues in boys' development from birth to manhood – and discusses the warm, strong parenting and guidance that boys need. He brings his humour, honesty and practical knowledge of families to the vital task of raising our sons.

Parents and teachers will find this a breakthrough book which changes their outlook on boys for the better, forever.

Printed by RR Donnelley at Glasgow, UK